Bloom's

GUIDES

Harper Lee's
To Kill a Mockingbird

1984
All the Pretty Horses
Beloved
Brave New World
Cry, The Beloved Country
Death of a Salesman
Hamlet
The Handmaid's Tale
The House on Mango Street
I Know Why the Caged Bird Sings
The Scarlet Letter
To Kill a Mockingbird

Bloom's
GUIDES

Harper Lee's
To Kill a Mockingbird

Edited & with an Introduction
by Harold Bloom

CHELSEA HOUSE
PUBLISHERS
A Haights Cross Communications Company

Philadelphia

© 2004 by Chelsea House Publishers, a subsidiary of Haights Cross Communications.

A Haights Cross Communications ⤴ Company

Introduction © 2004 by Harold Bloom.

Printed and bound in the United States of America.

First Printing
1 3 5 7 9 8 6 4 2

Library of Congress Cataloging-in-Publication Data

To Kill a Mockingbird / edited and with an introduction by Harold Bloom.
          p. cm. — (Bloom's guides)
Includes bibliographical references and index.
  ISBN 0-7910-7561-3 HC — ISBN 0-7910-7764-0 PB
  1. Lee, Harper. To kill a mockingbird. 2. Fathers and daughters in literature. 3. Race relations in literature. 4. Lawyers in literature. 5. Racism in literature. 6. Girls in literature. I. Bloom, Harold. II. Title. III. Series.
  PS3562.E353T6335 2003
  813'.54—dc21

                                        2003014153

Chelsea House Publishers
1974 Sproul Road, Suite 400
Broomall, PA 19008-0914

www.chelseahouse.com

Contributing editor: Mei Chin

Cover series and design by Takeshi Takahashi

Layout by EJB Publishing Services

Contents

# Introduction

HAROLD BLOOM

The continued popularity of *To Kill a Mockingbird* (1960), a generation after its initial publication, raises, without answering, the crucial question about the novel. Is it only a period piece, charming but now outdated, or does it possess something of the stuff of permanence? It came out of our last Age of Innocence, the Fifties, before the Vietnam War and the upheaval of the Counterculture, and long before our current crises of race relations, economic dislocation, and failure of faith in government, indeed in all authority. Rereading it returns one to an optimism about possibilities in human nature and in societal concern that many of us no longer share. Palpably, the book retains its pathos, but does it move us mostly through and by nostalgia? Is it now primarily a sentimental romance, touching but a shade childish, or is it, like J.D. Salinger's *The Catcher in the Rye*, another legitimate descendant of Mark Twain's *Adventures of Huckleberry Finn*, our classic romance of American childhood? Perhaps the questions can be summed up into one: Is Scout's narrative of her ninth year persuasively childlike, or is it essentially childish?

Jean Louise Finch, best known by her nickname, Scout, retains much of her charm as a classic American tomboy. She *is* indeed Harper Lee's book, being not only its narrator but much of its most interesting consciousness. Yet her deepest relation to Huck Finn, from whom she derives, is that like him she essentially cannot change. The crises of her book confirm her in her intrinsic strength and goodness, without wounding her sensibility or modifying her view of reality. Despite the villainous Ewell, and the conviction and death of the innocent Tom Robinson, a pure victim of Maycomb County racism, Scout retains not only her own idealism but her faith in the virtues of the people of her county. *To Kill a Mockingbird* comes out of an Alabama near related to William Faulkner's Mississippi, but in a cosmos apart from the world of *Light in*

August, As I Lay Dying, The Sound and the Fury, and the other Faulknerian masterworks. Clearly it would be foolish to measure *To Kill a Mockingbird* against the best American novels of our past century, but is it wholly invalid to use Faulkner's vision of reality as a standard for reality testing in regard to Harper Lee's novel? Is her view of human nature adequate to a mature sense of the complexities of our existence? I myself am uncertain of the answers to these questions, but depending upon which answers prove right, *To Kill a Mockingbird* will someday seem either a sentimental romance of a particular moment or a canonical narrative.

A formal critic could argue in favor of Harper Lee's aesthetic restraint, since how could we strictly expect traumatic change in so brief a span of time for a healthy nine-year-old girl? Yet the voice narrating the novel is that of the grown-up Jean Louise, studying the nostalgias of her ninth year and chronicling events clearly more remarkable than she has known since. Whatever life has brought her (and she tells us absolutely nothing about that), she evidently is fixated upon what could be termed the era of Bob Ewell and of Boo Radley, would-be murderer and heroic savior, in her life and in the lives of Jem and of Atticus. That far-off era is a time warp, with a foreground but no afterground, from which we are excluded. And yet we can surmise that Boo Radley's heroic intervention was a decisive turning point for Scout, persuading her permanently of the benign resources inherent in even the most curtailed and wounded human nature.

To Kill a Mockingbird is an impossible book not to like; you can reject its idealisms, but the portrait of Scout Finch will linger on in you anyway. There are palpable formulaic elements in the book; even its largest surprises seem predictable enough. Still, the book is refreshingly free of ideologies and of the need to revise history to suit some particular politics of the spirit. The book's permanent importance, or lack thereof, turns upon Scout's personality and character. She is neither Huck Finn battling for inner freedom while dreading solitude nor (in a lesser register) Holden Caulfield defending himself against breakdown and madness. Motherless, she yet has the best of fathers in Atticus and the best of brothers in Jem. Most of all, she has her self, a will-to-good so wholesome and open that it charms nearly everyone she encounters, short of the brutal Ewell and an officious relative or two. It is difficult to visualize a reader whom she will not charm, even at our time, in this place. Whether that charm will extend into days to come, I do not know.

Biographical Sketch

The youngest of four children, Nelle Harper Lee was born on April 28, 1926 to Frances Finch Cunningham Lee and Amasa Coleman Lee, a lawyer, in Monroeville, Alabama. One of Lee's childhood friends was Truman Capote, who would also become a celebrated novelist and essayist. She graduated from high school in Monroeville and then attended Huntingdon College, a private school for women in Montgomery, for a year (1944–45) before transferring to the University of Alabama. In 1947, she enrolled in the university's law school, later spending a year as an exchange student at Oxford University. She withdrew, however, in 1949, six months before she would have received a law degree and moved to New York City to pursue a writing career.

Lee had begun writing at the age of seven, and she had also written a variety of satires, reviews, and columns during her years in college. In New York, while working as an airline reservations clerk, she wrote several essays and short stories; none of these were published, but an agent encouraged her to expand one of the stories into a novel.

Receiving financial support from friends, Lee gave up her job and worked on the novel *To Kill a Mockingbird*, which was a fictionalized account of the Scottsboro Trial and would be her only book. Although she spent much time shuttling between New York and Monroeville tending to her ailing father, she finished a draft of the novel in 1957. An editor at the publishing firm J.B. Lippincott, Tay Hohoff, suggested revisions, and Lee rewrote the book. It was published in 1960.

To Kill a Mockingbird was an instant popular success, even though early reviews were mixed: some critics found the work too moralistic, while others found the narrative of Scout's girlhood to be corrupted by her adult sensibilities. A year after its publication, the novel had sold 500,000 copies and had been translated into ten languages. By 1982, more than 15,000,000 copies had been sold, and the book remains popular among students and the general public. It won a number of awards, including the Pulitzer Prize, the Alabama Library Association Award, and the Brotherhood Award of the National Conference of Christians and Jews. In 1962 it was adapted into a major motion picture in which Gregory Peck played the role of Atticus Finch. Lee was offered the chance to write the screenplay, but she declined; it was written by Horton Foote. The film won four Academy Awards, including best actor (Peck) and best screenplay (Foote). In 1970 Christopher Sergel's dramatic adaptation of *To Kill a Mockingbird* was published, and it has been performed widely throughout the United States and England.

Harper Lee has been very reclusive about her private life and about the sources for *To Kill a Mockingbird*. She has also written—or, at least, published—very little since the appearance of her novel, aside from a few pieces published in magazines, and a foreword written for the 35th Anniversary Edition of *To Kill a Mockingbird*. She gave considerable assistance to her boyhood friend Truman Capote in the research for his "nonfiction novel" *In Cold Blood* (1964), which is dedicated to Lee and Jack Dunphy. In June of 1966, Harper Lee was one of two persons named by President Johnson to the National Council of Arts. She has been awarded a number of honorary degrees, including a doctorate from the University of Alabama in 1990 and one from Spring Hill College in Mobile, Alabama in 1997. She continues to reside in Monroeville, Alabama.

The Story Behind the Story

To Kill a Mockingbird is set in the early 1930s during the Great Depression in the rural Southern town of Maycomb, Alabama. Despite Harper Lee's insistence that *To Kill a Mockingbird* is a work of fiction, certain places and characters bear a remarkable resemblance to those in Monroeville, Alabama, her hometown. Lee was born in 1926, which would make her exactly Scout's age ("almost six" at the start of the novel). Those who grew up in Lee's hometown remember one family's house, the Boulars, which was "boarded up and falling down" directly across the street from the Lee home, and the mysterious denizen named Sonny Boular, who almost certainly became the model for Boo Radley. Lee's father, Amasa Lee, was also a lawyer like Atticus Finch. It is therefore almost impossible to separate the novel, and most importantly, the precocious, tomboy character of Scout, from the author and her life.

Very little is known about the life of Harper Lee. She is famously reclusive and divides her time between New York City and Monroeville, and is rumored to be working on her second novel. She was born Nelle Harper Lee, the youngest of four children, to Frances Finch Cunningham Lee and Amasa Coleman Lee. She attended law school in Montgomery, but never finished; she also spent a year at Oxford, and worked behind the reservations desk at an airline. Since the publication of *To Kill a Mockingbird*, which took her eight years to write, the body of her published work has been limited to a few published essays in magazines. As far as her character is concerned, a glimpse of wryness is discernable in a handful of interviews conducted in the publicity frenzy surrounding the novel's 1960 publication, its 1961 Pulitzer Prize, and the subsequent 1962 film. For example, when asked, "Is it true your sister is a criminal lawyer?," Lee responded, "She's not a criminal, no."

But the most vivid depiction of Lee is through the recollections of her childhood friend, Truman Capote. Capote, who writes Lee into the slightly terrifying tomboy Idabel in his first novel *Other Voices, Other Rooms*, is himself immortalized as Dill in *Mockingbird*, and most biographers agree that no apter description of him as a boy exists than the one Lee conjures. Dill/Capote is a boy of almost psychotic imagination; a prophetic liar who is constantly inventing stories, many of them to explain his absent mother and father, in short:

> a curiosity. He wore blue linen shorts that buttoned to his shirt, his hair was snow white and stuck to his head like duckfluff; he was a year my senior but I towered over him ... a pocket Merlin whose head teemed with eccentric plans, strange longings, and quaint fancies.

Capote, in turn, remembers Lee as a girl who bullied boys, including himself. Lee's mother was an eccentric and a gossip who also tried to drown her in the bath at least twice, and while Capote found himself in trouble at the age of eleven when he published "Mrs. Busybody" in the local paper, perhaps Lee also borrowed elements from her mother to help create *Mockingbird*'s local nosy parkins Miss Stephanie. Lee and Capote were the best of friends, an effeminate, undersized boy and aggressive girl, both of them outcasts of their youth, sharing a precocious love of reading and a fascination with the goings on in Monroeville. Lee was a girl determined to have her own way. Moreover, when Capote set out for Kansas to report on the murders that would culminate in *In Cold Blood*, it was Lee who accompanied him. Indeed, it was Lee—tireless, garrulous, and accustomed to farm folk and their ways—who ultimately unlocked the tightly sealed lips of this small town. Apparently, Dill and Scout had not outgrown their morbid fancies. And it is reassuring to think that young Lee was probably just as stubborn as her doppelganger Scout, and that Scout the adult would maintain her liveliness.

Historical Background
On March 25, 1931, nine black men were arrested in Scottsboro, Alabama, accused of raping two white women on a train. The Scottsboro trials have become notorious, especially

in civil rights history. The women, Victoria Price and Ruby Bates, were mill-town females of dubious virtue, and it became increasingly apparent, especially after Bates withdrew her charges, that they leveled the accusation of rape to avoid being arrested for vagrancy. (They, and their two male companions, who were also their lovers, had stowed away on the train.) As is explained in *Mockingbird*, rape in 1930's Alabama was a capital crime and all defendants faced the death penalty. There was an overwhelming lack of physical evidence—Price, who had said that she was knocked on the head with a gun, beaten repeatedly, and raped by the nine men on a bed of spiky concrete, sported several small bruises on her backside, which, as the defending attorney and also the judge pointed out, could be caused by traveling, as the women did, in a coal carrier.

Nevertheless, all nine men were convicted, and there was a flurry of appeals that would continue, in fact, until 1973, when one of the defendants, Clarence Norris, who had been on death row, was pardoned. There are numerous parallels to the trial of Tom Robinson in *To Kill a Mockingbird*, not only in the blatantly unfair verdict rendered because of prejudice. There is also the issue of physical debilitation. One of the accused men in the Scottsboro trial was crippled, the other practically blind, and just as it was virtually impossible for Tom to have beaten Mayella with his withered left hand, it was also as impossible for these two men to have crossed the train and found their way to the coal car that Price alleged was the scene of the crime. Also, the dogged defense attorney Samuel Liebowitz, echoes the noble Atticus in his determination to acquit the nine men. Atticus, as well as the fictional Judge Taylor, are most indebted to the judge that presided over the Scottsboro trials, Judge James E. Horton. Judge Horton was virtuous, not unlike Judge Taylor, who, as Miss Maudie wisely points out, appointed Atticus particularly for the case. Or in her words, "Did it ever strike you that Judge Taylor naming Atticus to defend that boy was no accident?" Horton famously "put aside" a guilty verdict and hence ensured that he would not be voted in as judge the following year. Like Atticus, he outlines the overwhelming lack of evidence, and though Atticus's ultimate condemnation of

Mayella Ewell:

> I say guilt, gentlemen, because it was guilt that motivated
> her ... she struck out at her victim—of necessity, she must
> put him away from her—he must be removed from her
> presence, and from the world.

is considerably softer than Horton's closing remarks:

> History, sacred and profane, and the common experience
> of mankind teach us that women of the character shown
> in this case are prone for selfish reasons to make false
> accusations of both rape and insult upon the slightest
> provocation, or even without provocation for ulterior
> purposes.

it can't be denied that similarities exist between the real and
fictitious judges.

We also have to remember that *To Kill a Mockingbird* was
written in 1960 and published in New York. Perhaps some of
the reason for its immediate popularity is due to the fact that it
was not written in 1930's Alabama, whose unjust climate
provides the story's fuel, but rather, that it was written at the
height of the Civil Rights movement. Five years previous to its
publication, Rosa Parks refused to give up her seat on a bus in
Montgomery, Alabama. Martin Luther King, Jr., who was
already at the forefront of the movement, led the subsequent
Montgomery bus boycott and his house was bombed. Three
years before marked the beginning of court-ordered
desegregation of schools in Little Rock, Arkansas. In 1960,
tangible change was evident; *Mockingbird*, written during this
unstable time, looks back to an era when there was relative
calm. Some critics have argued *To Kill a Mockingbird* may not be
that radical of a book, because Harper Lee is critical of the past
but does not draw attention to the turbulence of the Civil
Rights movement. It was banned in some parts of the country,
primarily due to its references of rape and use of the word

"nigger," but otherwise drew accolades for its sympathetic portrayal of black characters. And Lee was allowed to continue her life in Monroeville—the town that *Mockingbird* condemns for its close-mindedness—in peace.

List of Characters

Known best by her nickname **Scout**, which implies a character of honest, indomitable curiosity, Jean Louise Finch remains one of the most endearing of child narrators and is generally assumed to be her creator's doppelganger. She is nearly six when the novel begins and almost nine when it ends. A tomboy, her mother dies when she is two; she has no girlfriends to speak of, and regards the womenfolk who are supposed to be her exemplars with a mixture of fear and awe. Scout distinguishes herself most prominently through her ferocious temperament and her inability to keep her thoughts to herself.

From the outset, we know that **Jeremy "Jem" Finch** will be his father's son—a future lawyer and gentleman who will carry on Atticus's legacy. A loner, he has a gentler personality than his firebrand sister, and yet his temper, when finally sparked, is a violent one indeed; he vandalizes Mrs. Dubose's camellias when she taunts his father. Scout's elder by four years, the novel is Jem Finch's passage to adulthood.

A fifty-something widower, attorney, and father of two, **Atticus Finch** is the undisputed hero of the book—the moral force of both the story and the town, and the quintessence of a Southern gentleman. But even Atticus's strengths are called into question when he is asked to defend Tom Robinson, a black man accused of raping a white girl.

Dill Harris first distinguishes himself by his diminutive size; he is a good year older than Scout but she towers over him. He is also a consummate liar, highly sensitive, physically unprepossessing, who comforts himself about his broken family by telling fantastic stories about his father, and spends the three summers with his aunt who lives in the Finch's neighborhood. It is general knowledge that he is modeled on Lee's childhood friend Truman Capote. Perhaps there is no more revealing moment than when Dill announces that he wants, when he grows older, to be a "clown."

Calpurnia or **"Cal"** is the most complicated and successful African-American character in the book. As the Finches' cook, she is as close to a mother as either Jem or Scout has ever known, except that she is harsher than a mother, but in many ways more idealistic. She is not a gentle woman, but as Atticus says, "She's tried to bring them [the children] according to her lights, and Cal's lights are pretty good." She is also, perhaps, an example of the potential for the African-American community—as one of its only members who can read and write, and though she recognizes her inferior position as a cook, Calpurnia rarely neglects to speak her mind.

Arthur "Boo" Radley is the shadow, the bogeyman, of the book. Boo only reveals himself at the end, though his presence provides much fodder for the children's imagination. It is rumored that he stabbed his father in the leg with scissors, and since that episode, he has never set foot outside the Radley house. Nevertheless, he leaves the children presents in the hollow of a tree and saves their lives—proving his human decency before vanishing for good behind the Radley threshhold.

A widow, **Miss Maudie Atkinson** grows azaleas and bakes the best cakes in town, but also provides guidance to the children; She is Scout's only real ladylike companion. Her character is a blend of shrewdness, humor, and compassion. It is typical of Miss Maudie to comment, as her house burns down, that she'd always wanted a smaller house anyway because it would give her a larger garden. Together with Atticus, she is the closest thing to the town's conscience.

Tom Robinson is the central victim of the story. A strong black man, he also has a shriveled left hand, which proves that he was unable to commit the crime of which he is accused—that of beating and raping Mayella Ewell—as the marks on her body indicate a left-hand perpetrator. He is condemned nonetheless, and then shot seventeen times when he attempts to escape.

Just as Atticus is the hero and Tom is the victim, so **Robert "Bob" Ewell** is the villain. And just as Tom is dangerously unnuanced in his role, so is Ewell, who is pure evil, of the drunken, lazy variety. A left-handed man, the evidence points that it was he who beat his daughter, and possibly raped her as well. ("She says she never kissed a growed man before ..." Tom reports about Mayella, "She says what her daddy do to her don't count.") Ewell later tries to kill the Finch children and is stabbed by Boo Radley in the attempt.

The epitome of southern graciousness and hospitality, **Aunt Alexandra** is Atticus's older sister who stays with the Finch family in the summer of the trial. Though Scout initially resents Aunt Alexandra's attempts to turn her into a little lady, she ultimately respects Aunt Alexandra for defending Atticus's character.

Mayella Ewell is Bob Ewell's daughter who accuses Tom Robinson of rape, even though it is clear that her father has abused her.

Heck Tate is the upstanding sheriff of Maycomb who always tries to do right by the citizens. He is also a witness at Tom's trial.

The son of a poor farmer, **Walter Cunningham** is one of Scout's classmates whom the Finch family invites to dinner.

Mr. Walter Cunningham is a poor but decent farmer who initially is part of the mob that wants to kill Tom, but changes his mind at the persistence of Scout.

Mrs. Henry Lafayette Dubose is a cantankerous elderly woman who lives near the Finches. Though she angers Jem by insulting his father, he learns that Atticus respects her because she is honest and courageous in battling a morphine addiction.

Summary and Analysis

To Kill a Mockingbird consists of two parts and three distinct sections connected by devices that are sometimes successful, and sometimes haphazard. Part one includes chapters one through eleven and is arguably the most powerful and coherent section of the book. The second section, which includes chapters 12–25, details Tom Robinson's trial and subsequent death. The third section, also in part two, is a quick effort to draw all the elements of the plot together, and happily so. It details Maycomb after Tom's death and the aftermath of the trial. Most importantly, it describes how Scout and Jem are attacked by Bob Ewell on their way home from their school pageant.

The first section of the book (**chapters 1–11**) is primarily about Southern childhood, but it heavily foreshadows the events in parts two and three—the small dramas in part one will be magnified later in Tom's trial. Scout opens by explaining, "When he was nearly thirteen, my brother Jem got his arm badly broken at the elbow"—the point to which the book will eventually return, so that we are not taken in by the initial, contented, almost lazy pace.

A hodgepodge of characters are introduced, each with their own manner of speaking and odd traits. Among the adults alone these include bespectacled Atticus; dotty Miss Maudie; chatterbox Miss Stephanie; hearty Heck Tate; domineering Calpurnia who taught her son—the local garbage collector— to read from Blackstone's *Commentaries*; and sour Mr. Avery, whose hobby is to whittle stockwood into toothpicks. Also introduced is Maycomb, so vivid with personality that it is almost a character in itself. Maycomb is a "tired old town" where doors are never locked and everyone knows each other's business. It is also implied that Maycomb has a mildly incestuous reputation; out in the neighborhood of Old Sarum, "the Cunninghams married the Coninghams until the spelling of the names was academic—academic until a Cunningham disputed a Coningham over land titles and took to the law."

Similarly, among gentlefolk, Atticus is "related by blood or marriage to nearly every family in the town."

The first few pages of *To Kill a Mockingbird* contain some of its most descriptive writing:

> In rainy weather the streets turned to red slop, grass grew on sidewalks, the courthouse sagged in the square. Somehow it was hotter then ... Men's collars wilted by nine in the morning. Ladies bathed before noon, after their three o'clock naps, and by nightfall were like soft teacakes with frostings of sweat and sweet talcum.

This is a child's imaginative vision recalled with adult grace. Though Scout's perspective is never corrupted, Lee does not condescend by making her sound infantile.

Scout and Jem are the only children of the town lawyer, Atticus Finch. Atticus is middle-aged and a widower, and his children are often paranoid about the manliness of their father. He doesn't hunt like the other men in town, nor does he "play poker, fish, drink or smoke." He has never remarried, which sparks taunts from vindictive townspeople like Mrs. Henry Lafayette Dubose. Nor has he ever physically punished his children. From the beginning, the reader is aware that Atticus is heroic, but he is far from redeeming himself as a hero in his children's eyes. "Atticus," Scout tells us, "was feeble: he was nearly fifty," and he didn't "do anything that could possibly arouse the admiration of anyone." Far more authoritative, at least in Scout's eyes, is the Finch's black cook Calpurnia, who reads and forces Scout to practice penmanship, and also slaps her at will. Yet the children are terrified of Atticus's judgment, without knowing exactly why. Or in Jem's words, "Atticus ain't ever whipped me as far as I can remember. I wanna keep it that way."

Dill Harris arrives in Maycomb to spend the summer with his aunt, and he quickly reveals a natural ability to tell lies; he and the Finch children become fast friends. For approximately the first fifty pages of the novel, we are shown how idyllic life in Maycomb can be. Certainly small-mindedness exists, and while Maycomb is an old town, its courage is placed in question as being one of the only towns left undamaged by the Civil War. It is the height of the Depression, and everyone is poor; yet in this enclosed, impoverished, sweltering world, children can play. Doors are always open and neighbors pay social calls every Sunday. "People," Lee explains, "moved slowly then," and such a pace gives the young room to invent games, run rampant on the town streets, and stay safe.

Indeed, that first summer with Dill is delightful, especially because there is nothing that can make a child's paradise more complete than a mystery. Maycomb citizen Boo Radley is that mystery, who lives in the boarded-up "droopy and sick" house and never comes out, who is rumored to have stabbed his father with a pair of scissors and scatters poisoned pecans in his yard. The children incorporate the mystery of Boo Radley into their games; they dare each other to touch Boo's front door, try to write him letters, and devise their own mini-plays that they perform on the street. While children may be enchanting creatures, Lee is firm in her conviction that they are not wholly innocent. They would be bored, after all, with swapping comics and reenacting King Kong and Tom Swift. Danger adds an element of unpredictability to their lives.

Scout's first day of school marks the start of action in what has been so far a somewhat indolent book. Scout is not emotionally equipped to deal with the tribulations of everyday life, as the action in the classroom demonstrates. She is humiliated by the teacher because she can already read—she is bored—and then, as a final blow, she is rapped on the knuckles with a ruler. These schoolroom scenes contain some of the most endearing moments in the book: the naive teacher, Miss Caroline who insists on the "Dewey Decimal" system of education and faints at the sight of cooties; and the overgrown kids who have repeated the first grade already three times. Miss Caroline reading this raggedy bunch of children a story about cats in "cunning little clothes" is almost as entertaining as the vision of her waving cards printed with words like "cat" "rat" "man" and "you." "... [T]he class," Scout explains, "received these impressionistic revelations in silence."

All the white children in Maycomb attend the same school, and children of sharecroppers and the lowliest residents share blackboards with children of lawyers, which was standard practice in 1930's Alabama. Camille Maxwell Elebash remembers, "I always took two lunches, one for myself, one for someone else." (Johnson, 147) At the age of six, Scout is faced with the challenge of fitting in, and it is not a prospect that she relishes. In addition, Walter Cunningham, the son of a poor farmer, is invited to dinner with the Finch family and pours syrup over his entire supper. Later, Calpurnia slaps Scout (who has brought this table manner to loud attention) for Walter, despite his hookworms and bare feet, is decent enough to be the Finches' "comp'ny"; though his father is poor, he is different from many of the dubious characters that share his economic bracket. His father, Mr. Cunningham, never has the money to pay for services, but he will repay in potatoes and stockwood. His family is honest and hardworking, if ignorant and broke, and they deserve to be treated with respect. The only other significant episode during the school year is that Boo Radley has started leaving the children presents in the oak tree—Double-Mint gum, Indian head pennies, a broken gold watch.

The following summer, Scout establishes a friendship with their neighbor Miss Maudie Atkinson, who, despite her eccentricity, is proud and well-bred in her own way, meriting of people's respect; together with Atticus and Calpurnia, she establishes herself as another mouthpiece for right. Later, Dill, Jem, and Scout try to break into the Radley house. In the shooting that follows, Jem loses his trousers on the barbed wire fence, and when he returns in the middle of the night to retrieve them, finds them stitched and folded neatly over the fence.

The next winter, snow falls, and this is significant because it is a strange occurrence for Maycomb and a foreshadowing of events to come. Jem makes a snowman out of mud and piles snow on top, essentially a "nigger snowman" that he has whitened, but symbolic because it signifies how shallow the divisions of color actually are. Furthermore, he first makes the snowman into a caricature of their neighbor Mr. Avery, and then, at Atticus's suggestion, adds Miss Maudie's hat. Whether the snowman is now a woman or a man becomes ambiguous. That night, the coldest night in Maycomb, opposites coincide once again as Miss Maudie's house catches fire and, despite the snow, flames consumes her precious azeleas. Unnoticed, Boo Radley slips outside and covers the shivering Scout with a blanket.

For Christmas, Jem and Scout are given air rifles. In perhaps what is the most obviously significant exchange in the first section (conversational exchanges will increase after chapter 12) Atticus tells them that "it's a sin to kill a mockingbird."

The action moves to February, when Atticus shoulders a rifle and kills a mad dog in one shot. It is a deeply pregnant moment, emphasized by the still trees and the silenced mockingbirds, and Atticus's emasculating spectacles falling to the ground and breaking. For the first time in Maycomb, the doors are closed tightly. Only Calpurnia has latched and then unlatched the screen door in anticipation. Just as he will do for Tom Robinson, Atticus stands alone in confronting madness for the sake of the town. And the madness is only more menacing because it is quiet. In Scout's words, "I thought that mad dogs foamed at the mouth, galloped, leaped, and lunged at throats ... Had [the dog] behaved thus, I would have been less frightened." Yet despite its leaden symbolism, this episode is redeemed by the children's response. They had no idea Atticus could even wield a gun up until this point, and he is now a hero in their eyes. Before he can prove his virility to them by virtue in the courtroom, he first must prove it on a physical level

In another episode, Jem tears down Mrs. Henry Lafayette Dubose's precious camellias, his response when she insults his father, "Your father's no better than the niggers and trash that he works for!" First Miss Maudie's azaleas are ruined, and then Mrs. Dubose's Snow-on-the-Mountains. Everywhere flowers—a symbol of everything feminine and genteel in the South—are being destroyed. There is no more fitting symbol of landed Southern womanhood, of course, than the camellia, and in ravaging Mrs. Dubose's bushes, Jem, essentially, is attacking her heritage and her pride. Jem's penance, enforced rather mysteriously by Atticus, is to read to her from *Ivanhoe* every Sunday. In the end, Mrs. Dubose dies, and Atticus reveals that the weekly reading was the way that Mrs. Dubose had weaned herself from a morphine addiction. She leaves Jem a camellia, a symbol that her old South will endure despite how he might try to angrily knock it down; and even after her death we are left perplexed as to why Atticus triumphs her and refuses to let his enraged son throw the blossom upon the fire. Hovering, of course, over these later episodes is the one momentous event that will propel the story from being an ordinary catalogue of the quirky day-to-day into high drama. Atticus has been appointed to defend a black man, Tom Robinson, who has been charged with raping a white girl, Mayella Ewell.

If there is one consistency in the novel, it is that the children, throughout, are learning to distinguish between hearsay and the truth. As Atticus claims, "I just hope that Jem and Scout come to me for their answers instead of listening to the town." However, it is interesting that the children first find out about the case through gossip. Atticus, noble man that he is, sometimes behaves in perplexing ways. He allows Scout to overhear his conversation with Uncle Jack, but he rarely confronts his children about the issue—or, indeed, any issue. This is Atticus's way; the children have to ask him first. Perhaps this is why the children are not aware of the magnitude of the things to come at the end of part one. And perhaps this is also why Scout escapes the end of the book relatively unscathed. Jem and Dill, older and far more deeply sensitive, will be wounded. But Scout lacks the understanding to be truly hurt by what happens—and no one gives it to her. Though three years older than at the beginning of the novel, she emerges from the story with the innocence still typical of a nine year old. What matters most is defending her honor—which is still wounded quickly, but never permanently—and surviving school.

The events of section two (**Chapters 12–25**) are less episodic and more melodramatically charged. By the time Calpurnia takes Jem and Scout to the local black church, Tom Robinson's trial is imminent. Here, Scout learns that everyone with the exception of four members in the black community—including Cal and her son Zeebo—is illiterate, a shock to someone for whom reading was so natural that it never occurred to her how she may have learned it, since Cal was instrumental in teaching Scout to write. In the short time leading up to the trial, Scout learns a great deal about race relations.

Several events occur that propel the action in the pivotal second section of the novel. Dill returns to Maycomb—he has left Mississippi and his unfeeling parents. In a small, yet poignant moment, Scout realizes what it might feel like to be unloved. Lack of love is not just being chained in the basement, as Dill first claims his mother and stepfather have done. "... they do get along better without me, I can't help them any. They ain't mean.... They kiss you and hug you good night and good mornin' and good bye and tell you they love you." Dill feels Maycomb is the only place where he is valued. Scout, on the other hand, is always needed in a way that she has just begun to understand.

Also at this point in the novel Aunt Alexandra suddenly takes command of the household. Alexandra, who in Scout's recollections often resembled a battleship and gave her an "add-a-pearl necklace," is not a welcome addition to Scout's life with her ideas that little girls should play with tea sets. Scout can feel the walls of a "pink cotton penitentiary" closing in. And curiously enough, Atticus does not object to her presence—in fact, he doesn't even inform the children that she is coming. In his mystifying way, he explains that Scout must obey her, must obey him, and must obey Calpurnia, even though the three perspectives rarely coincide. It is as if seven-year-old Scout is thrust into a perpetual contradiction. But Atticus, in the end, is always right. Ultimately, Alexandra's behavior upon hearing of Tom's death will be a study of majesty, and will make Scout realize that the true Southern lady is not simply artifice.

The trial of Tom Robinson is famous. Whether or not it accurately represents the judicial proceedings in Southern small towns at the time is not certain—from the hysterics of the witnesses and a judge who calls both attorneys by their first names and looks as though he is about to fall asleep when he is not munching his cigar (he doesn't light it but consumes it to its tip and then spits the whole mess out), to Atticus's lengthy and powerful conclusion. It is, however, one of the purest and most perfect examples of a mistrial. Not only is there no existing medical evidence to support that Mayella Ewell has actually been raped, but Mayella has bruises that could only have been inflicted by someone left-handed. Her father is left-handed, and it becomes increasingly apparent that Mayella is a victim of her father's sexual advances. The blatant injustice of the trial, coupled with Lee's great character sketches, is a testament to her superior story telling abilities.

In many ways, the pre-trial is more sordid than the deliberate miscarriage of justice that follows. The families—both black and white—picnic on fried chicken, sardines, and Coca-cola around the courthouse; this trial to them is a fête, as it is the most exciting thing to happen in Maycomb in years. But the reason this scene is so powerful is because the reader witnesses it through Scout's eyes, with a child's sense of anticipation and eagerness of this "gala occasion," even though to an adult with a sense of moral decency it is quite appalling. "It's like a Roman carnival," sneers Miss Maudie, who declines to attend. Thus the dichotomy between the childhood fantasy world of Scout and the actual events of the trial demonstrates the ugliness of the situation.

Right before the trial commences, an incident occurs in which Scout disperses an angry mob that has assembled at the county jail to lynch Tom. In this scene, Atticus is standing guard over Tom Robinson's cell, and just as the children happen upon him, the men approach. For a while, violence seems inevitable as the mob grows more impatient. Then, Scout singles out Mr. Cunningham—tenant farmer, client of Atticus, and father of her aforementioned schoolmate Walter—from the crowd, and questions him about Walter. Failing that, she pursues the topic of entailments.

Atticus had said that it was polite to talk to people about what they were interested in, not what about you were interested in. Mr. Cunningham displayed no interest in his son, so I tackled his entailment as a last ditch effort to make him feel at home.

Just minutes before, Scout has kicked the man who has laid a hand on her brother. "Barefoot," she explains, "I was surprised to see him fall back in real pain. I intended to kick his shin, but aimed too high." Moments like this lighten the tense scene. W.J. Stuckey, who dismissed *Mockingbird* as "self-consciously cute" points out the scene's key faults. Its climax, Stuckey states, revolves around Mr. Cunningham doing "a particular thing"—"these are rhetorical tricks resorted to by fiction writers when they are unable to cope with the difficult problem of rendering a scene dramatically. The author wants Mr. Cunningham to have a change of heart ... but she is unable to bring it off ..." (Stuckey, 194). Furthermore, Stuckey notes that Mr. Cunningham has not, until then, been distinguished as a leader in any way, so the act of him calling off the mob with the wave of the hand is somewhat dubious. Dramatically, the scene is flawed; yet it sparks a reaction in the reader. And despite the fact that Stuckey might call Scout accidentally kicking an aggressor an example of Lee's "cuteness," it is a poignant moment in the scene. Atticus sums up why Scout and Finch have rescued him that night: "You children last night made Walter Cunningham stand in my shoes for a minute." If they did, it was through laughter and lightness. The humor of youth not only saves Atticus, and temporarily Tom, it also saves the scene itself for the dearest moments of *Mockingbird* are those that make us chuckle. "Laughter," Lee explains, about an earlier confrontation between Atticus and the gentlefolk, "broke them up." Scout's humor, which springs from her mulish, pared down notions, is arguably the most skilled element in the book. Lee manages to make Scout's humor seem effortless, which lifts a moral melodrama above mawkishness.

The trial encompasses **chapters 16–20**, of which Tom's powerful testimony is considered to be the book's climax; both succinct and colorful, in many ways it is almost too humble and credible. He not only describes what happened on November 21st—the day of the alleged rape—but also provides pivotal information about Mayella Ewell. "She says she never kissed a grown man before an' she might as well kiss a nigger," Tom says, "She says what her papa do to her doesn't count." Even though Tom Robinson's testimony is near perfect, certain factors compromise this scene. First, the book has transformed from childhood nostalgia story to "morality play;" critic R.A. Dave, who has nothing but praise for the book, says that the courtroom narrative "is in the danger of getting lost in the doldrums of discussion—dull, heavy, futile." (Dave, 56)

To Kill a Mockingbird is not a consistent book. As Granville Hicks points out, it "is not primarily about the childhood experience," for Lee has the bigger issue of "the perennial Southern problem" on her mind. Her challenge, in Hicks's mind, "has been to tell the story she wants to tell and stay within the consciousness of a child." (Bloom, ed., 5) There is not one story in *To Kill a Mockingbird*, but several, and the principal plot line is one that is too morally weighty for a child of nine to comprehend. Hence, in an effort not to compromise Scout's childlike perspective, Lee has put the rather weighty aspects of her tale into the mouths of her adults. The adults, therefore, in part two, become noticeably less endearing. In part one, Atticus is certainly already an idealist, and yet he is also a wry widower engaged in the honest struggle of raising two children on his own. In part two he is a mouthpiece for justice. And surely there is nothing more disappointing than the batty, yet unquestionably elegant Miss Maudie launching into a speech:

> "The handful of people who say that fair judgement is not marked White Only; the handful of people who say a fair trial is for everybody, not just us; the handful of people with enough humility to think, when they look at a Negro, there but for the Lord's kindness am I."

Granted, Miss Maudie, like Atticus, has shared her wisdom

throughout the novel, but it has been within her character—slightly obscure in meaning and always dry. This speech is not conversation, but a sermon.

There is not much that is artless about *To Kill a Mockingbird*. Actions are deliberate—Atticus shooting the rabid dog, Calpurnia taking the children to the black church. Only the children, especially Scout, are really natural in this symbol-laden world, and their naturalness is never better expressed than it is with Scout's wondering voice.

If we are devastated by Tom's fate, therefore, it is because earlier, we have laughed at characters and their actions that may have played a role in it. The warmth that permeates the book, that even frames Tom's trial—before with Miss Maudie calling after Miss Stephanie, "Better be careful he doesn't hand you a subpoena" and immediately after with the grinning Atticus threatening to eat pickled pork knuckles in the dining room underneath his prim sister's nose—is turned on its head.

There is even slapstick during the trial itself. When the prosecuting attorney objects that the defense is "browbeating" the witness, the Judge snorts, "Oh sit down, Horace, he's doing nothing of the sort. If anything, the witness is browbeating Atticus." In this instance, however, the only person to laugh is the Judge. The rest of the courtroom is so silent that Scout wonders whether the babies have been "smothered at their mother's breast." This is the same sort of silence that greeted Atticus upon shooting the wild dog. Such a cessation of laughter is chilling, for what we have accepted as humorous is amusing no longer. Though the judge cracks jokes, doors are left unlocked, and children are allowed to ramble free at all hours of the night, intimacy comes with a price—narrow-mindedness. Suddenly, small town generosity curdles as quaint Maycomb habits reveal their menace, and one realizes that the price of little freedoms is suffocation on a grand scale. Those who sense it most acutely, it appears, are the most innocent members—the infants.

The trial is the one event of the book when we get little sense of Scout's thought process. Her role in the trial episode is as reporter; somehow her young mind is able to recall everything that was done and said. This is an adult arena, and she provides little commentary, except when Atticus loosens his clothing to prepare for his final address: "... he unbuttoned his vest, unbuttoned his collar, loosened his tie and took off his coat ... to Jem and me, this was the equivalent of him standing before us stark naked." But such a comment is only to underscore the symbolic significance of this gesture. Atticus is like a gladiator or a boxer stripping before a fight, or even more so, like a sacrifice in preparation to be slaughtered for the common good.

Jem and Dill feel the trial's pain most acutely; in many ways Scout is too young to comprehend the gravity of the situation. As Jem tells Reverend Sykes, "I think it's okay, Reverend, she doesn't understand it." It is telling that of the three children, Scout alone does not shed tears. Dill runs out during the prosecution's cross-examination—the treatment of a human being with such a lack of respect makes him sick to his sensitive soul. Jem cries later that night. But it is precisely because the rest of the trial is so fun for them that its conclusion is devastating—they sneak away and break the rules to attend; they sit upstairs with Reverend Sykes and the rest of the blacks, which is the greatest adventure of all. Indeed, the scene in which the children await the verdict is well orchestrated. The children are truly heady with excitement; not only have they attended the most important event in Maycomb history, they have also been caught and have gotten away with it. Despite Calpurnia's protests, Atticus lets them return to the courtroom after supper. "I was exhilarated," Scout recounts, "So many things had happened so fast I felt it would take years to sort them out ... what new marvels would the evening bring?" No one stops to wonder whether it is right to feel so giddy when a man's life is at stake. Such giddiness behooves youth alone.

Ultimately, it will be Jem who is cut the deepest by the trial's conclusion, for he is the oldest. Already, we bleed for him when he burbles, "We've won, haven't we?" because he is setting himself up for heartbreak. When Tom is pronounced guilty, Scout is dizzy; but Jem, who remains hyper-conscious, weeps through the night and cannot eat the next morning. Scout's daze is engendered from her lack of understanding and the fact that she has, just minutes before, woken up from a nap on the Reverend Sykes's shoulder. Jem, on the other hand, finds himself confronted for the first time with the wrongs of the world. He is just sophisticated enough to grasp hatred with its fullest implications, and is too vulnerable not to be shaken. As he says to Scout later, "I think I'm beginning to understand why Boo Radley's stayed shut up in the house all this time ... it's because he *wants* to stay inside."

Dramatically, the most accomplished and certainly subtlest episode in part three is the Missionary Ladies Society's tea party hosted by Aunt Alexandra at the Finch house. The ladies of Maycomb, who, for the most part, stay silent during the book, come alive in these few pages; notably Mrs. Merriweather, who, only stops her offensive dither to recharge, and Mrs. Farrow, "the second most devout lady" who speaks with "a soft sibilant sound," which in Lee's rendering means that she speaks like a snake. Very little actually happens here, for this is the bewildering "world of women," where "fragrant ladies rocked slowly, fanned gently, and drank cool water" and the action lies in the subtext. This is the only time in the novel that the characters say exactly what they don't mean. Yet the tension is so evident that even six-year-old Scout senses it; it is also a tension so dense that one cannot see, move, or breathe. In Scout's words, "Ladies in bunches always filled me with vague apprehension and a firm desire to be elsewhere." It turns out that her apprehension is well justified and not just the everyday restlessness of a little tomboy. Ladies in bunches are *evil*.

Unlike the men of Maycomb, the women cast an opaque web over the world. Their role in the novel is to obfuscate, whereas Scout has grown up under the tutelage of Atticus, whose purpose in life is to cast light and make things clear. Men tend not to "trap you with innocent questions to make fun of you," whereas the ladies delight in other people's distress. Considering that nothing deliberately important is done or said at the tea, Lee draws the scene out almost indulgently.

The ladies have gathered to proclaim their indignation at the squalid life lead by the Mrunas, in Africa. This is a classic ironic device: morally overblown people that cast their attentions to the troubles in exotic lands so that they can shut their eyes to the troubles at home. Mrs. Merriweather states what is in many ways the motto of Maycomb: "Well I always say forgive and forget, forgive and forget ... If we just let them know we've forgiven 'em, we've forgotten it, then this whole thing will blow over." The citizens of Maycomb have always willed themselves to forget anything unpleasant, which is why they will never learn.

During the tea party, Mrs. Merriweather insults Atticus, but in the backhanded way of the Maycomb women. "Now far be it for me to say who, but there's some of 'em in this town thought they were doing the right thing a while back, but all they did was stir 'em up." At this point, Miss Maudie snaps. She herself is schooled in feminine double-speak, so she retorts in a way that is suitably difficult to understand. "His food doesn't stick going down, does it?" she remarks, referring to Atticus's untainted conscience. Her words are lost on Scout entirely. But the gaze of gratitude that Alexandra gives Maudie is not lost on her young niece; it is a blazing gesture of honesty in a cold, untruthful environment.

Atticus arrives home in the middle of the tea party with news of Tom, who is shot to death while attempting to escape from prison. Alexandra and Maudie, together with Calpurnia, find themselves united, and this time not by glances and ladylike double entendre. When Alexandra calls Atticus "brother," Scout realizes that she has arrived in the household, not for reasons of her own, but for the sake of the family, and most importantly, for that of her younger sibling. Miss Maudie, rather significantly, unties Calpurnia's apron for her as she prepares to go to the Robinsons. In the end, Miss Maudie and Aunt Alexandra clean their faces and resume their church tea party as if nothing has happened—all of the time, with their hearts plagued, but deriving strength from the other's presence.

Such an alliance—between Miss Maudie and Aunt Alexandra, who up until now could not have been more different—is somehow more poignant, and certainly more thoroughly realized, than Mr. Cunningham calling off the lynch mob with a wave of his hand. This, for more than anyone else, is Aunt Alexandra's moment. She has never consciously been a champion for right—what concerns her is propriety and background. But her devotion to Atticus, though unstated, is pure, and it is that devotion that opens her eyes. "It tears him up," she says, a woman who cannot fully express her emotions, yet loves her brother all the same, "... [This town] is perfectly willing to let him do what they're afraid to do themselves." She still might not understand the right that Atticus is trying to represent, but she does acknowledge her little brother as a hero. And with those words, Alexandra takes a stand and redeems herself.

The third section (**chapters 26–31**) of the novel is not openly indicated, but there is a clear break in the action between chapters 25 and 26. Just as Atticus has feared, Maycomb returns swiftly to normal. "Maycomb," Lee writes, "was interested in the news of Tom's death for perhaps two days." The Maycomb inhabitants have resumed their habit of examining injustices abroad—Adolf Hitler has taken control of Germany. In **chapter 26**, a schoolteacher who had earlier commented about how the blacks were getting above themselves, lectured the children about the wrongs of Nazi Germany and prejudice. As Scout says, "... how can you hate Hitler so bad an' then turn around and be ugly about folks right at home...."

Then the setting shifts ahead to one evening in October, when there is a Halloween pageant and Scout is to appear with the third grade dressed as a ham. Mortification sets in early, for Scout falls asleep backstage, misses her cue, and is scolded by her teacher. Scout mistakenly assumes that this is the worst thing that can happen to her that night. However, while walking home from the pageant, Jem and Scout are beset by Mr. Bob Ewell, who attacks them with the intention to kill. But they are mysteriously rescued. Scout escapes with a few scratches and Jem is carried home unconscious with the same broken arm described in page one, and Mr. Ewell is discovered dead with a knife in the ribs. Their hero turns out to be the children's alleged bogeyman, Boo Radley, and the story has come full circle. Mr. Bob Ewell pays for Tom Robinson's death with his own life. Most importantly, his end serves as a memorial to Tom in a town that has forgotten him. And the one remaining victim of vicious gossip, Boo, has revealed himself as not only very much a human being, but as the savior of children.

Most critics have described the concluding segment as the weakest, mixing disparate elements—political commentary, slapstick humor, and violence—in a sequence of events that proceeds at a frenetic pace. Indeed, Lee seems to be rushing to tie up loose ends, and certainly the ending of *Mockingbird* is more surreal than anything that has preceded it. But there are glimpses of the same magic that infected the early third of the book. Some critics have argued that the events of Halloween are unbelievable, but in many ways they ring truer than Atticus's speech to the courtroom, or Scout confronting the lynch mob. Much of what transpired at the Halloween party was taken from actual events.

During Lee's childhood in Monroeville, young Truman Capote threw a Halloween party in which many of the entertainments mirrored those in *Mockingbird*—the children bob for apples, and they also put their hands into cardboard boxes to touch mystery substances. What was significant was that Capote had invited both a black man and also the reclusive Sonny Boular, who as previously stated, most likely provided Lee with the model of Boo. The Ku Klux Klan threatened to invade, and eventually laid their hands on Sonny, who was making a rare appearance completely unrecognizable in a robot costume of cardboard and wire. The Klan, thinking they had found the black man they set out to find, was on the verge of hanging Sonny and the sheriff was nowhere to be found. Interestingly enough, it was Harper Lee's attorney father— Amasa Coleman Lee, allegedly the original Atticus Finch— who stopped the Klan and humiliated them. According to Marianne Moates's account of Capote's Monroeville years, *A Bridge to Childhood*, he said, 'You've scared this boy half to death because you wanted to believe something that wasn't true. You ought to be ashamed of yourselves." (Moates, 62) Purportedly, behind Amasa Lee stood the prominent citizens of the town, just as the sheriff Heck Tate and Judge Taylor would eventually stand behind Atticus. Of course, the truth of such memories is colored by the fiction that they have inspired—we have no idea how much the events of Capote's party have hence been confused with the events in *Mockingbird*. Nevertheless, it demonstrates how sometimes the commotion of real life is often wilder than fiction. In real life, misery, sweetness, and violence, do often occur in the same breath. Halloween in *Mockingbird* is a queer night, but it feels less contrived than much of the book precisely because it is so strange.

Mockingbird also closes with a hint of uneasiness, which is unusual for a book that, up until this point, has been secure in its convictions. When Atticus believes that it is Jem, now unconscious and unable to say what happened, who is responsible for Mr. Ewell's death, he seems willing to try his teenage son. True, this is also the man who would guard over his son all night and "would be there when Jem waked up in the morning." But Atticus mulls over whether Jem will be tried before the county court: "Best way to clear the air is to have it out in the open ... I can't live one way in town and another way in my home." He is the man with such a good heart, such a just conscience; his balanced sense of right makes him incapable of the tenderness that possesses most fathers. When Sheriff Heck Tate insinuates that it is Boo, and not Jem, who is the guilty party, the dialogue reverses direction. For Tate ultimately convinces Atticus to state that Ewell fell on his knife, and Atticus turns his back from the central force in the book and in his life—the law. This is the man who once claimed that the beauty of the court lay in its ability to make all men equal, that it was the "one human institution that makes the pauper the equal of a Rockefeller, the stupid man the equal of an Einstein, and the ignorant man the equal of any college president." In the final pages of *Mockingbird*, this institution appears to be fallible. Its fall is foreshadowed when Jem shouts, "I don't wanta hear about that courthouse again, ever, ever, you hear me?"—a cry from a boy who has always looked up to the law. In the end, even Atticus has to own that though the law is a great equalizer in theory, there are men who are superior to it, and can make decisions without it. These do not include the Ewells, they do not even include honest farmers like Mr. Cunningham; it is an elite circle which seems to include Atticus and Heck Tate only.

The dialogue between the sheriff and Atticus is, as in several other passages in the book, obscure. One has a better sense reading it quickly; once it is subjected to scrutiny, it becomes confusing—there are too many gaps, too many insinuations, too many seemingly irrelevant statements. But the attack scene is also baffling in the same way; we don't know what is happening because we are only experiencing it from Scout's point of view—terrified for her life and half-blind in her ham costume. Similarly, Atticus and Tate's talk is reported from her ears only. In many ways, it reads much more like the memory of an eavesdropping little girl than, say, her account of Tom Robinson's trial. She does not quite comprehend the whole, but she gets a sense of the important points.

Joyfully, Lee lets us become children again in part three; we have returned to her fantastic and sometimes merciless fairy-tale world. But where in the beginning children acted out adventures in their imaginations, the happenings in part three are arguably satisfying because they are a children's adventure in the flesh. The denouement—Boo stepping into the light—is true to this storybook quality. Granted, it is not the most believable moment, but after the somber events of the trial and its aftermath, there is something refreshing about the ogre stepping out of the castle and revealing himself as a prince. These last ringing moments are gloriously true to Scout, who, after all, is still a little girl who believes, even after the past three years, that "nothin's real scary, except in books." So there are no grand adult moral statements to finish *To Kill a Mockingbird*, just the observation that "there wasn't much else to learn, except algebra." The melancholy that haunts these last few pages is poignant because it seems birthed from a genuine child's understanding.

Neighbors bring food with death and flowers with sickness and little things in between. Boo was our neighbor. He gave us two soap dolls, a broken watch and chain, a pair of good luck pennies, and our lives. But neighbors give in return. We never put back into the tree what we took out of it; we had given him nothing, and it made me sad.

Small children don't feel tragedies on a large scale, they experience tragedy through the people and things with which they are intimate, and then rebound with incredible resilience. Scout's lesson, her "coming of age" moment, if you will, is appropriate to being eight-years-old.

In tone, and particularly concerning the central drama of Tom Robinson, the book is triumphant rather than tragic. This is despite Tom's death, and not just because Ewell receives his comeuppance at the end. Atticus has fought on the side of right and, in his own way, has won. He never thought that he would win the trial in the first place, but there was always the possibility of an appeal and most importantly, it had opened the eyes of this sleepy town for an instant. Though Tom is convicted, the black community still honors him; they stand in unison as he passes. The jury is out for a few hours rather than the few minutes that Atticus is expecting. The fact that there are other people in Maycomb who are on the side of right is also a small victory—happily, as Miss Maudie points out to Jem, they include society's most important figures—the local judge and sheriff. There is also a Cunningham on the jury—one of the same men who had tried to lynch Tom just days before—who is "rarin'" for a complete acquittal. As Jem says, "One minute they're tryin' to kill him and the next they're tryin' to turn him loose." Then there is the Maycomb reporter Braxton Underwood, who, in Atticus's words, "despises Negroes ... he won't have one near him." Nonetheless, just as Maycomb has almost forgotten Tom's death, Underwood writes a lengthy editorial in which he compares "Tom's death to the senseless slaughter of songbirds by hunters and children." Also, most of Maycomb might have forgotten Tom, but "Tom was not forgotten by his employer Mr. Link Deas." The person who benefits from this is Tom's widow. Deas hires her as a cook, but also confronts and threatens Bob Ewell when he tries to harass her. Ultimately, it is Bob Ewell who really loses. Even though he has received the guilty verdict that he demanded, he gains none of the respect that he was hoping the verdict would bring him, just as Price and Bates had hoped during the Scottsboro trials. "... [H]e'd thought he'd be a hero," says Atticus. Instead he is publicly humiliated, sent back to his squalor, and if anything, more despised than before. No one listening to the testimony could doubt that he is the guilty party. Even after Tom's death, Atticus can still be tickled by the expression on Judge Taylor's face. "I proved him a liar but John made him look like a fool ... John looked at him as if he were a three-legged chicken or a square egg." If Maycomb forgets Tom Robinson, they also forget Bob Ewell, and all his lunatic attempts to keep himself remembered are just laughed at by the genteel community that he hates.

The film version of *Mockingbird* (1962), which is by and large faithful to the spirit of the book, turns Tom's death into the central tragedy for which there is no redemption except Bob Ewell's death—a sort of poetic justice. Needless to say, Ewell's death is fate, whereas the true triumphs in the book are born of purposive human accomplishment. The intent of Atticus to fight for Tom, and that of Link Deas to protect Helen Robinson, are *Mockingbird's* victories, covered in the novel but skipped in the film. One reason there is such a discrepancy between the film and the book's treatment of Tom's death is the timing of events. In the movie, Tom's death immediately follows the verdict. Atticus and his children are walking home from the trial when they hear the news. There is no time to reflect, no time for the black community to cram the Finch kitchen with scuppernongs and pickled pigs feet, most especially, no time to understand the little ways in which Atticus wins. Though Tom's death is called "senseless" in the book, it does bring some sense to the town, and *Mockingbird* makes this clear in glancing ways. But the movie has to strip these intimations. We are left instead with the plain fact of an honest man murdered down without good reason, leaving a wife and children behind.

"This may be a shadow of a beginning," Atticus says, and that is all he can hope for in Maycomb. What he considers a victory in the courtroom is telling of the time period in which the novel is set. Leaving a jury out for hours when before they would have been out for minutes—even if they deliver a guilty verdict in the end—is rare occurrence for 1930's Alabama. The movie, on the other hand, is much more attuned to the turbulent 1960's spirit. Tom's conviction, and ultimately his death, can be nothing short of horrible. It is in these glimpses of a beginning, these barely perceptible sunbeams that are overlooked by people and certainly not bright enough to be captured on celluloid, that are the triumphs of the literary embodiment of Atticus Finch. Fortunately, he is an astute enough a man to recognize them himself.

Social implications: Race, Class, and Gender

To Kill a Mockingbird illustrates the effects of prejudice on society. In Maycomb, the blacks ride in the back seats, live on the outskirts of town, have segregated sections in public spaces, and come into contact with white folks only in their jobs as cooks, trash collectors, and cotton pickers. As far as their church is concerned, "Negroes worshiped in it on Sundays, and white men gambled in it on weekdays." But prejudice is not limited to race. *Mockingbird* addresses all types of bigotry—those engendered by class, sex, and religion. Scout will never grow to be anything but a lady, though she wears overalls in childhood. And a lady is not necessarily a great thing to become. Jem taunts Scout by calling her Angel May when she is reluctant to break into the Radley house, saying, "I declare to the Lord, you're gettin' more like a girl every day!" Similarly, Aunt Alexandra will not have young Walter Cunningham come around to the Finches for supper because he is "trash." While blacks keep their separate quarters, so tenant farmers dwell in the woods, and the "white trash" beyond that—in the "dump" where they live in ugly, filthy hovels. And while men may better themselves spiritually in *Mockingbird*, it is nearly impossible to improve socially.

Even the best of people are allowed their prejudices. Miss

Maudie, slightly crazy like some of the Maycomb gentlefolk, may respect Boo Radley, but places the blame on "Old Mr. Radley" and his "footwashing Baptist" ways. This is an example of resentment characterized by Christian superiority. The view is that everyone should be a practicing Christian and attend church, for Christianity is as much a social practice as it is a sacred one—indeed, there are many sects in white Maycomb, and they are all friendly, with the ladies from all sects congregating for tea. One should not worship at home or carry beliefs to the extreme, both of which the Radleys are guilty. Atticus, who, it seems, can look kindly upon a lynch mob, is satisfied with the way the townspeople tell Bob Ewell to "... get back to your dump." Indeed, Miss Maudie's behavior in her garden is a perfect metaphor for her and Atticus's attitude towards the community:

> She loved everything that grew in God's Earth, even the weeds. With one exception. If she found a blade of nut grass in her yard, it was like the Second Battle of the Marne, she swooped down upon it with a tin tub and subjected it to blasts from beneath with a poisonous substance she said was so powerful it'd kill us all if we didn't stand out of the way.

Miss Maudie hates nut grass because one sprig can contaminate an entire yard, just as a weed like Bob Ewell can poison a town. Hence, the most generous of human beings—in this case Atticus and Miss Maudie—have their "one exception." For this, Lee does not condemn them. There is always one danger that no one can overcome. And it is telling that both Miss Maudie's and Atticus's prejudices—against "footwashing Baptists" and "white trash" respectively—are appropriate to the convention that *To Kill a Mockingbird* endorses.

For in many ways, *To Kill a Mockingbird* is deeply conventional—albeit liberally conventional—for its time. Lee did not write her novel in Alabama, she wrote it in New York City at a time when it was not uncommon for liberal college educated elites—from the North and the South both—to take an interest in African-American rights. Most of the outrage the book engendered was due to its focus on rape, and not to its sympathetic portrayal of blacks. Ironically, there was outrage from the African-American community itself, for the novel's free use of the word "nigger," though Lee portrays black characters in a sympathetic light.

Race relations had always been a problem for the South, but there was also an increased paranoia about the poor white class. The South was decaying still, but its decay was blamed on white poverty infiltrating the genteel classes. Prevalent in *Mockingbird* is what is commonly called the "New South question." Fred Erisman, in his essay, "The Romantic Regionalism of Harper Lee," eloquently argues that Lee believes that the New South is only possible if it incorporates "the New England romanticism of an Emerson." (Erisman, 46) But Lee believes also in the mores of the Old South—not its bigotry, but its tradition, dignity, and romance. Maycomb stews in a "narcisstic regard for the warts and pimples in the past" (Erisman, 48) in part because it has lost its pre-Civil War pride. Erisman may believe that Lee advocates a breakdown of the class structure she details in *Mockingbird*, but in many ways *Mockingbird* upholds it. The reader should note that those who lobby for racial change are upper-middle class: notably Atticus Finch and Judge Taylor, who appoints Atticus to defend Tom. Tolerance, therefore, can only come via such men—products of genteel background; it does not come from the farmers and certainly not from the "white trash." In fact, the elites are essential to resolving not only the race problem, but the problem of the South itself.

To Kill a Mockingbird demonstrates that there are two kinds of gentility in the world—inherited and natural. Young Chuck Little, for instance, may be six years old and not know "where his next meal was coming from," but in Scout's words, he is "a born gentleman," and even a hulking brute like Burris Ewell respects him. Similarly, Calpurnia is a lady, and Tom Robinson's manners are "as good as Atticus's." Nevertheless, Chuck Little is still a tenant farmer's son who will never have Scout Finch over for supper, and Tom, even to Atticus, is still a "boy," even though he has a wife and three children. Nineteen-year-old Mayella is a "woman." To call a grown black man a "boy" was to judge him inferior to white men and women, which many people believed at this time.

The Finches descend from a noble background; not only are they born to it, but they carry themselves as such. The upper class is also populated with Mrs. Merriweathers and Miss Crawfords, who may have inherited an advantage but do not conduct themselves with propriety. Mrs. Dubose, on the other hand, is a different case altogether. She may not be the friendliest of human beings—indeed she is a cantankerous, bigoted annoyance—but when Atticus sends Jem over to read to her on her deathbed, he is not just doing it out of pity, for Atticus actually holds Mrs. Dubose in high esteem. Mrs. Dubose, during her last few months, was a morphine addict; Jem's weekly sessions helped her wean her off her addiction. "You know," Atticus tells Jem, "she was a great lady ... According to her views, she died beholden to nothing and nobody. She was the bravest person I ever knew." Mrs. Dubose is the Old South, represented by the camellias that she grows—fragrant, tradition-bound, and waxy as death. She may represent the South's prejudice and its ugliness, but also its pride and willpower. Atticus may see the promise of the New South in his children, for they, in their innocence and openness, represent the kind of New England romanticism that critic Fred Erisman discusses; but he sees Mrs. Dubose as necessary to that New South as well.

Another character integral to the rise of the New South is Dolphus Raymond, the local eccentric who rarely comes into town and carries with him a brown paper bag that smells of whiskey. Cloaked by a similar aura of mystery that surrounds Boo Radley, he lives in the colored quarters with his black mistress and mixed children, and rumor has it that he is an "evil man." In the end, however, Raymond reveals himself as a drinker of Coca-cola rather than of whiskey, and also as a source of wisdom. He pretends to be an alcoholic because "it's mighty helpful to folks ... they could never, never understand that I live like I do because that's the way I want to live." He understands about "the simple hell people give other people—even without thinking."

Raymond takes a different approach from Atticus in society. Rather than taking a stand for what is right, he hides; it is what ultimately makes Atticus a nobler man because, unlike Raymond, Atticus is "the same man in his house as he is on public streets." Yet there is something endearing about Raymond, peacefully living with his bi-racial family, in many ways living the same way that Calpurnia has instructed Scout: "It's not necessary to tell all you know ... when they don't want to learn there's nothing you can do but keep your mouth shut ..." It goes without saying that this man is also its largest landowner, and his breeding is so evident that Scout can smell it. "I liked his smell," she confesses, "it was of leather, horses, cottonseed. He wore the only English riding boots I had ever seen." In certain ways—his dress, his black mistress, and brood of mixed children—he has the bearing of gentleman slave owners of yore. On the other hand, he is probably Maycomb's most radical citizen, and a perfect example of mixing new ways with the old.

Dolphus Raymond can live the way he wants because he is rich. Maycomb's poor, on the other hand, have no such choice. But while the tenant farmers try to maintain their decency, there is another class—that of the "white trash"—that is simply irredeemable. This is already clear in the first grade classroom when Burris Ewell spits at the teacher and calls her "a snot-nosed slut." It is as if the "white trash" attitude is knit into these people at birth—a rather harsh assertion for what has been such a compassionate book. According to Atticus, "you never really know a man until you stand inside his shoes and walk around in them." Atticus can forgive a lynch mob; he can even tell his children not to hate Hitler. But Atticus does not step inside Bob Ewell's shoes, let alone try. A poor white man like Bob Ewell is Atticus's "one exception." He cannot be saved.

Social status in *Mockingbird* is a lifelong classification; you can work to improve your station, but you can not transcend it. This is part of Mayella Ewell's downfall—she has lofty ambitions of rising above her station. Bob Ewell may want the town's attention, but Mayella wants more. She wants to be a dignified Southern lady. In lieu of this wish, she grows geraniums, "cared for as tenderly as Miss Maudie Atkinson had Miss Maudie Atkinson deigned to permit a geranium on her premises." Geraniums are not a lady's flower, but they make Mayella's pathetic effort to imitate her betters all the more poignant. Victoria Price and Ruby Bates in Scottsboro were cleaned up for court—these women of dubious virtue were bathed, dressed, and perfumed to look like gentlewomen, so that their purported rape would seem an attack on the ladylike chasteness that was such a bastion of Southern identity. Similarly, Mayella in court "looked as though she tried to keep herself clean" and seems "somewhat fragile-looking," but as she seats herself she becomes what she is—"a thick-bodied girl accustomed to strenuous labor."

Despite Atticus's assertion that the court system is our great social evener, at the end of *Mockingbird*, it is clear that the public courts may not hold the answer to everything. Hence, when Bob Ewell is stabbed, the "good" Heck Tate and Atticus Finch look away. People with the breeding to know, can in fact, serve Justice; and looking after the town is the responsibility of upstanding citizens. Shouldering such responsibility is a complicated business, and is similarly laden with conduct codes and rules as having "compn'y." Having someone over for "compn'y" is a subtle way of asserting superiority, because one can afford to extend graciousness; hence, guests can behave however they like, but the hosts must have manners. The Finches can have Walter Cunningham to supper, but the Cunninghams will never have the Finches. Scout is slapped because she is rude to young Walter at the dinner table, when she is expected to behave with the propriety becoming a hostess. This also explains why Alexandra is upset when Cal takes the children to her church, and why she forbids Scout to be Cal's guest ever again, for Cal has tipped the social balance by playing the hostess. Calpurnia, in the church, forbids Jem to contribute to the collection plate with his own money. But the hierarchy between the children and Cal is gently restored when Jem proffers his and Scout's money the second time the collection plate comes around. Men like Atticus are like benevolent hosts, and Maycomb is their permanent company. It is of the utmost importantance for Atticus and his children to conduct themselves with grace.

After Tom's trial, Jem says to Scout, "There are four kinds of folks in the world. There's the ordinary kind like us and the neighbors, there's the kind like the Cunninghams out in the woods, the kind like the Ewells down at the dump, and the Negroes." Scout concludes, after a lengthy discussion, "Naw Jem, I think there's just one kind of folks. Folks." Jem responds, "That's what I thought, too, when I was your age." It is a simple scene, disarming because moral issues are being debated from a child's perspective. It is also a narrative crux. Scout's argument is from the innocent's perspective—what we want to be true but we know is not. Jem is wiser; he is beginning to realize that there are stratifications in this world, which cause hate, and the only hope for those who want to make a difference is to learn how to operate within the system.

Born as they are to the Maycomb upper class, Jem will grow up to be a gentleman and Scout to be a lady, and they both must take on the duties that their respective roles require. While we have a pretty good idea of what is expected of Jem from his father's legacy, Scout's future is less clear; but in many ways, it's just as demanding. For Southern ladies are crucial to the backbone of Maycomb. This is not to say that *Mockingbird* is a feminist text. As previously stated, Jem is encouraged to be a lawyer while Scout is not. (Lee, incidentally, attended law school in Alabama and her older sister became one of the most widely recognized attorneys in the South.) And Atticus cheerfully remarks that if women were allowed on juries, "I doubt if we'd ever get a case tried—the ladies'd be interrupting to ask questions." But aristocratic Southern women are a formidable presence in *To Kill a Mockingbird*, and if Scout has a quest in the novel, it is in recognizing the true ladies from the false, and in appreciating a true lady's value.

Ladylike conduct comes with an overwhelming number of rules that often contradict one another, and is expected to be instinctive. Naturally, tomboy Scout, who is without girlfriend, sister, or mother, is revolted by what she regards as her "pink cotton penitentiary" fate. She is bewildered and frightened by her Aunt Alexandra's teaching. Being a lady, in Scout's mind, seems to entail not wearing pants, not associating with "trash,"

> playing with small stoves and tea sets and wearing the Add-A-Pearl necklace she gave me when I was born; furthermore that I should be a ray of sunshine in my father's lonely life.

When Scout, quite reasonably, points out that she can be a ray of sunshine in overalls as well as skirts, Aunt Alexandra cannot provide her with a satisfactory answer, so she scolds Scout instead. What Scout realizes by the end, however, is that being a lady is something that is at once simpler to understand and more challenging to undertake. It is about being subtle and modest while maintaining one's integrity. As Cal tells her, "It's not necessary to tell all you know. It's not lady like."

Not until the Missionary Ladies tea party does Scout arrive at this realization. Mrs. Merriweather and the ladies of Maycomb may outwardly depict the refinements of Southern womanhood, with their glossy nails and murmured voices; Scout had always associated them as feminine paradigms; but the ladies of Maycomb are vindictive, spiteful creatures. Scout comes to learn that there is a difference between restraining oneself and being dishonest, between gentle criticism and virulent stabs in the back. A true lady does not insult her hostess's brother when he is not there to defend himself, as Mrs. Merriweather does. Kinship is forged between Aunt Alexandra and Miss Maudie when they recognize each other as the only other women of character on the porch:

> Aunt Alexandra got up from the table and swiftly passed the refreshments, neatly engaging Mrs. Merriweather and Mrs. Gates in brisk conversation. When she had them well on the road to Mrs. Perkins, Aunt Alexandra stepped back. She gave Miss Maudie a look of pure gratitude and I wondered at the world of women.

Later, Scout sees Aunt Alexandra pull herself together with Miss Maudie's curt assistance, and smilingly returns to passing out teacakes. A true lady never exposes herself, but inside, she remains true amongst the hypocrites. Mrs. Dubose is ultimately a great lady and Mrs. Merriweather is not, for Mrs. Dubose is honest. And to carry on despite a broken heart, as Aunt Alexandra does that afternoon, can be as courageous as shooting a mad dog on a February day. For the first time, Scout is suitably impressed: "... if Aunty could be a lady at a time like this, so could I."

If the principal players in *Mockingbird* are men, the most powerful presence is feminine—that of the South herself. Indolent, sweltering Maycomb is more like the Missionary Society ladies than any of the men in the town—always thinking one thing, saying another, wanting to forget, never wanting to move. The South has always been represented as a woman, stereotypically symbolized by magnolias and Scarlett O'Hara.

Rape is a central element to *Mockingbird* because Southerners are sensitive about the subject of violation, especially since their landscape was plundered during the Civil War. Hints of rape are characteristic throughout the novel; the subject is not limited to Mayella Ewell's circumstances. The razing of Miss Maudie's azaeleas by fire and of Miss Duboses's camellias by Jem are examples of rape symbolism (Tellingly, Miss Maudie, who personifies the promise of the New South, springs back with optimism, while Miss Dubose, the old South, is thirsty for revenge.) the citizens of Maycomb are eager to blame Mayella's rape on Tom Robinson because they want to blame the Old South's decay on the black population. That the perpetrator is obviously Bob Ewell is telling of Lee's own class paranoia: poor whites of dubious character, or "white trash," and not blacks, are responsible for the "rape" of the Southern way of life.

Works Cited

Dave, R.A. "Harper Lee's Tragic Vision," *Modern Critical Interpretations: To Kill a Mockingbird*. New York: Chelsea House Publishers, 1998.

Erisman, Fred. "The Romantic Regionlism of Harper Lee," *Modern Critical Interpretations: To Kill a Mockingbird*. Chelsea House Publishers, 1998.

Hicks, Granville. "Three at the Outset," *Modern Critical Interpretations: To Kill a Mockingbird*. New York: Chelsea House Publishers, 1998.

Johnson, Claudia Durst. "Interview: A Perspective on the 1930's," *Understanding To Kill a Mockingbird*. CT: Greenwood Press, 1994.

Moates, Marianne M. *A Bridge of Childhood*, H. Holt, 1989.

Stuckey, W.J. *The Pulitzer Prize Novels: A Critical Backward Look*. University of Oklahoma Press, 1966.

Critical Views

In her first novel, *To Kill a Mockingbird*, Harper Lee makes a valiant attempt to combine two dominant themes of contemporary Southern fiction—the recollection of childhood among village eccentrics and the spirit-corroding shame of the civilized white Southerner in the treatment of the Negro. If her attempt fails to produce a novel of stature, or even of original insight, it does provide an exercise in easy, graceful writing and some genuinely moving and mildly humorous excursions into the transient world of childhood.

Set during the depression, the story is recalled from the distance of maturity by Jean Louise ("Scout") Finch, whose widowed father, Atticus, was a civilized, tolerant lawyer in a backward Alabama town. An older brother, Jem, and a summer visitor from Mississippi, Dill, share Scout's adventures and speculations among figures not totally unfamiliar to readers of Carson McCullers, Eudora Welty, and Truman Capote.... [The children] play their games of test and dare with ill-tempered old ladies, buzzing village gossips, and, most especially, with the mysterious occupant of the house next door who has never been seen outside since his father locked him up over fifteen years earlier. It is through Boo Radley whose invisible presence tantalizes the children, that Miss Lee builds the most effective part of her novel: an exploration of the caution and curiosity between which active children expend their energies and imaginations.

In the second half of the novel, Atticus defends a Negro accused of raping a white girl. The children add to their more innocent games that of watching a Southern court in action. They bring to the complexities of legal argument the same luminous faith in justice that sweeps through their games, and they watch, with dismay and pain, as the adult world betrays them. And here, perhaps because we have not been sufficiently prepared for the darkness and the shadows, the book loses strength and seems contrived. For everything happens as we might expect. The children are stained with terror and the knowledge of unreasoning hatreds but gain in insight and in compassion, and the author, deliberately using Atticus and an elderly widow as mouthpieces, makes her points about the place of civilized man in the modern South.

The two themes Miss Lee interweaves throughout the novel emerge as enemies of each other. The charm and wistful humor of the childhood recollections do not foreshadow the deeper, harsher note which pervades the later pages of the book. The Negro, the poor white girl who victimizes him, and the wretched community spirit that defeats him, never rise in definition to match the eccentric, vagrant, and appealing characters with which the story opens. The two worlds remain solitary in spite of Miss Lee's grace of writing and honorable decency of intent.

NICK AARON FORD ON THE PORTRAYAL OF AFRICAN AMERICANS

To Kill a Mockingbird by Harper Lee, born and bred in Alabama, is the complete antithesis of *Seed in the Wind*. Instead of stereotyped Negroes, this novel presents living, convincing characters—neither saints nor devils, neither completely ignorant or craven or foolish, nor completely wise or wholly courageous. Instead of blatant propaganda from beginning to end, the socially significant overtones do not begin to appear until the story has progressed a third of the way and then they creep in unobtrusively, as natural as breathing.

The story is really about a white Alabama lawyer named Atticus Finch and his efforts to raise his young son and daughter in such a way that they will always seek to know right from wrong and when they have discovered the right, or the truth, to live by it regardless of the cost. In his efforts to practice the creed he has adopted for himself and his children, he is faced with the task of defending a Negro falsely accused of raping a white girl. The most exciting part of the book deals with the temporary hate aroused against himself and his children in the typically Southern community as he steadfastly seeks and presents the truth of the case to the dismay of those who do not wish to accord the Negro equality before the law. Although his client is convicted, notwithstanding conclusive evidence to the contrary, and later killed attempting to escape the jailers, his action in the face of intimidation, abuse, and violence against himself and his children finally arouses such a sense of decency in the community that it would be unlikely that another such travesty of justice could ever happen there.

The story is told by Jean Louise Finch, Atticus' daughter, aged six at the beginning and eight at the end. It is dominated by the daughter's complete love and devotion for her father and older brother, her admiration for a boy her own age, her acceptance of Negroes as fellow human beings with the same rights and privileges as those of white people, and her hatred of all hypocrisy and cant. Her dramatic recital of the joys, fears, dreams, misdemeanors, and problems of her little circle of friends and enemies gives the most vivid, realistic, and delightful experiences of a child's world ever presented by an American novelist, with the possible exception of Mark Twain's *Tom Sawyer* and *Huckleberry Finn*.

The author's contribution to a healthy social sensitivity among her readers is twofold. Indirectly it reveals itself in the quiet dignity and wisdom of the Finch's cook and housekeeper, Calpurnia, in her dealings with the children of the household and the white and Negro adults of the community; in the antisocial, uncultured conduct of white school children, as well as adults, of low socio-economic status; in the conversion of aloof, undemonstrative citizens to active participation in the struggle for elementary human rights when abuses become flagrant and unbounded. It is revealed directly in such passages as the following, which quotes Atticus' comment to his thirteen-year-old son who is greatly disturbed because a jury has convicted an innocent Negro:

The one place where a man ought to get a square deal is in a courtroom, be he any color of the rainbow, but people have a way of carrying their resentments right into a jury box. As you grow older, you'll see white men cheat black men every day of your life, but let me tell you something and don't you forget it—whenever a white man does that to a black man, no matter who he is, how rich he is, or how fine a family he comes from, that white man is trash.

FRED ERISMAN ON THE REGIONALISM OF THE SOUTH

Throughout *To Kill a Mockingbird*, Harper Lee presents a dual view of the American South. On the one hand, she sees the South as still in the grip of the traditions and habits so amply documented by Davis, Dollard, and others—caste division along strictly color lines, hierarchical class stratification within castes, and exaggerated regard for kin-group relations within particular classes, especially the upper and middle classes of the white caste. On the other hand, she argues that the South has within itself the potential for progressive change, stimulated by the incorporation of the New England romanticism of an Emerson, and characterized by the pragmatism, principles, and wisdom of Atticus Finch. If, as she suggests, the South can exchange its old romanticism for the new, it can modify its life to bring justice and humanity to all of its inhabitants, black and white alike.

In suggesting the possibility of a shift from the old romanticism to the new, however, Miss Lee goes even further. If her argument is carried to its logical extension, it becomes apparent that she is suggesting that the South, by assimilating native (though extra-regional) ideals, can transcend the confining sectionalism that has dominated it in the past, and develop the breadth of vision characteristic of the truly regional outlook. This outlook, which Lewis Mumford calls a "soundly bottomed regionalism," is one that "can achieve cosmopolitan breadth without fear of losing its integrity or virtue: it is only a sick and puling regionalism that must continually gaze with enamored eyes upon its own face, praising its warts and pimples as beauty marks. For a genuine regional tradition lives by two principles. One is, *cultivate whatever you have*, no matter how poor it is; it is at least your own. The other is, *seek elsewhere for what you do not possess*; absorb whatever is good wherever you may find it; *make it your own.*" If the South can relinquish its narcissistic regard for the warts and pimples of its past, it can take its place among the regions of the nation and the world.

Miss Lee sees such a development as a distinct possibility. Maycomb, in the past isolated and insulated, untouched by even the Civil War, is no longer detached from the outside world. It is, as Miss Lee suggests through the Finch brothers' going elsewhere to study, beginning to seek for what it does not possess. (This quest, however, is no panacea, as Miss Lee implies with the character of the pathetically inept Miss Caroline Fisher, the first-grade teacher from North Alabama, who introduces the "Dewey Decimal System" to revolutionize the Maycomb County School System.) Moreover, Maycomb is being forced to respond to events touching the nation and the world. The Depression is a real thing, affecting the lives of white and black alike; the merchants of Maycomb are touched by the fall of the National Recovery Act; and Hitler's rise to power and his persecution of the Jews make the power of Nazism apparent even to the comfortable Christians of the town. Maycomb, in short, like the South it represents, is becoming at last a part of the United States; what affects the nation affects it, and the influence of external events can no longer be ignored.

The organic links of Maycomb with the world at large extend even further, as Miss Lee goes on to point out the relationship between what happens in Maycomb and the entirety of human experience. The novel opens and closes on a significant note—that life in Maycomb, despite its Southern particularity, is an integral part of human history. This broadly regional vision appears in the first paragraphs of the novel, as the narrator, the mature Scout, reflects upon the events leading up to the death of Bob Ewell:

I maintain that the Ewells started it all, but Jem, who was four years my senior, said it started long before that. He said it began the summer Dill came to us, when Dill first gave us the idea of making Boo Radley come out.

I said if he wanted to take a broad view of the thing, it really began with Andrew Jackson. If General Jackson hadn't run the Creeks up the creek, Simon Finch would never have paddled up the Alabama, and where would we be if he hadn't? We were far too old to settle an argument with a fist-fight, so we consulted Atticus. Our father said we were both right.

The theme of this passage—that events of long ago and far away can have consequences in the present—is echoed at the novel's end. Tom Robinson is dead, Bob Ewell is dead, Boo Radley has emerged and submerged, and Scout, aged nine, is returning home. The view from the Radley porch evokes a flood of memories, which, for the first time, fall into a coherent pattern for her: the complex interaction of three years of children's play and adult tragedy is revealed in a single, spontaneous moment of intuitive perception. "Just standing on the Radley porch was enough," she says. "As I made my way home, I felt very old.... As I made my way home, I thought what a thing to tell Jem tomorrow.... As I made my way home I thought Jem and I would get grown but there wasn't much else left for us to learn, except possibly algebra." She has learned, with Emerson, that "to the young mind everything is individual.... By and by, it finds how to join two things and see in them one nature; then three, then three thousand; and so, tyrannized over by its own unifying instinct, it goes on tying things together ... [discovering] that these objects are not chaotic, and are not foreign, but have a law which is also a law of the human mind." When the oneness of the world dawns upon a person, truly all that remains is algebra.

Miss Lee's convictions could not be more explicit. The South, embodied here in Maycomb and its residents, can no longer stand alone and apart. It must recognize and accept its place in national and international life, and it must accept the consequences for doing so. It must recognize and accept that adjustments must come, that other ways of looking at things are perhaps better than the traditional ones. Like Emerson's individual, it must be no longer hindered by the name of goodness, but must explore if it be goodness. If, to a perceptive and thoughtful observer, the old ways have lost their value, new ones must be found to supplant them; if, on the other hand, the old ways stand up to the skeptical eye, they should by all means be preserved. This Atticus Finch has done, and this he is teaching his children to do. By extension, the South must do the same, cultivating the good that it possesses, but looking elsewhere for the good that it lacks. Only in this way can it escape the stifling provincialism that has characterized its past, and take its place as a functioning region among human regions. If the South can learn this fundamental lesson, seeking its unique place in relation to human experience, national experience, and world experience, all that will remain for it, too, will be algebra.

R.A. Dave on Tragic Elements

The novelist, in an unmistakable way, has viewed one of the most fundamental human problems with the essentially Christian terms of reference, and we see emerging from the novel a definite moral pattern embodying a scale of values. As we notice the instinctive humanising of the world of things we are also impressed by the way Harper Lee can reconcile art and morality. For *To Kill a Mockingbird* is not a work of propaganda, it is a work of art, not without a tragic view of life. The novelist has been able to combine humour and pathos in an astonishing way. But comedy and tragedy are, in the final analysis, two sides of the same coin. The novel bubbling with life and overflowing with human emotions is not without a tragic pattern involving a contest between good and evil. Atticus in his failure to defend the Negro victim, eventually hunted down while scaling the wall in quest of freedom, the innocent victim, and Arthur Boo, who is endowed with tender human emotions and compassion, but is nearly buried alive in the Radley House, which is a veritable sepulchre, simple because his father loved to wallow in the vanity fair, and the suffering Finch children, they all intensify the sense of waste involved in the eternal conflict. 'The hero of a tragedy,' observes Freud in *Totem and Taboo*, 'had to suffer; this is today still the essential content of a tragedy.' By that norm, *To Kill a Mockingbird* could be seen to hover on the frontier of a near-tragedy. The tragic mode is no longer a monopoly of the theatre. Like the epic that precedes it, the novel that succeeds it, too, can easily order itself into a comic or a tragic pattern. Particularly after the seventeenth century, tragedy seems to be steadily drifting towards the pocket theatre. *To Kill a Mockingbird* has the unity of place and action that should satisfy an Aristotle although there is no authority of the invisible here as in a Greek tragedy. With Atticus and his family at the narrative centre standing like a rock in a troubled sea of cruelty, hatred and injustice, we have an imitation of an action which is noble and of a certain magnitude. And the story, that is closed off on the melancholy note of the failure of good, also is not without its poetic justice through the nemesis that destroys the villain out to kill the Finch children. In fact, twice before the final catastrophe the story seems to be verging on its end. The first probable terminal is chapter twenty-one, when Tom is convicted and sentenced; the second is chapter twenty-six, when Tom is shot dead—not killed but set free from the coils of life, as it were and there is nothing really left. But the novelist wants to bring the story to a rounded-off moral end. Like a symphony it starts off on a new movement after touching the lowest, almost inaudible key, and we have the crescendo of its finale. Here is exploration, or at least an honest attempt at exploration, of the whole truth which is lost in the polarities of life. But Harper Lee who lets us hear in the novel the 'still, sad music of humanity' is immensely sentimental. Her love for melodrama is inexhaustible. Hence, although her view of human life is tragic, the treatment is sentimental, even melodramatic. However, though not a tragedy, it is since *Uncle Tom's Cabin* one of the most effective expressions of the voice of protest against the injustice to the

Negro in the white world. Without militant championship of 'native sons' writing in a spirit of commitment, here is a woman novelist transmuting the raw material of the Negro predicament aesthetically.

William T. Going on Scout's Point of View

Maycomb and the South, (...) are all seen through the eyes of Jean Louise, who speaks from the mature and witty vantage of an older woman recalling her father as well as her brother and their childhood days. This method is managed with so little ado that the average reader slips well into the story before he realizes that the best evidence that Atticus has reared an intellectually sophisticated daughter is that she remembers her formative years in significant detail and then narrates them with charm and wisdom. She has become the good daughter of a good man, who never let his children know what an expert marksman he was until he was forced to kill a mad dog on their street. Atticus did not like to shoot for the mere sport of it lest he kill a mockingbird like Tom Robinson or Boo Radley; and mockingbirds must be protected for their songs' sake.

This modification of a Jamesian technique of allowing the story to be seen only through the eyes of a main character but to be understood by the omniscient intelligence of Henry James is here exploited to bold advantage. The reader comes to learn the true meaning of Maycomb through the eyes of a child who now recollects with the wisdom of maturity. Along with Scout and Jem we may at first be puzzled why Atticus insists that Jem read every afternoon to old Mrs. Henry Lafayette Dubose in atonement for his cutting the tops off her camellia bushes after she taunted him about his father's being "no better than the niggers and trash he works for." But we soon learn with Scout that Atticus believed Jem would become aware of the real meaning of courage when he was forced to aid a dying old woman in breaking the narcotic habit she abhorred.

Jean Louise's evolving perception of the social milieu in her home town as she grows up in it and as she recalls her own growing up involves the reader in an understanding of the various strata of Maycomb society and its Southern significance. After Jem has brooded about the trial, he explains to Scout that

> There's four kinds of folks in the world. There's the ordinary kind like us and the neighbors, there's the kind like the Cunninghams out in the woods, the kind like the Ewells down at the dump, and the Negroes.
>
> "What about the Chinese, and the Cajuns down yonder in Baldwin County?"
>
> "I mean in Maycomb County. The thing about it is, our kind of folks don't like the Cunninghams, and the Cunninghams don't like the Ewells, and the Ewells hate and despise the colored folks."
>
> I told Jem if that was so, then why didn't Tom's jury, made up of folks like the Cunninghams, acquit Tom to spite the Ewells?

After considerable debate Scout concludes, "Naw, Jem, I think there's just one kind of folks. Folks."

This naively sophisticated sociological rationalization is far more valid and persuasive in its two-pronged approach. As mature readers we realize its mature validity; as observers of children we delight in their alert reactions to the unfolding events. The convolutions of the "mind of Henry James" have given way to the immediacy and pithy wisdom of Jean Louise's first-person narration.

W. J. STUCKEY ON THE NOVEL'S DEFECTS

As a first novel, *To Kill a Mockingbird* is better than average. Despite its simplistic moral, some early scenes (in the school room especially) are well executed even though they are self-consciously cute. A rather long scene toward the close of the book (the meeting of Aunt Alexandra's church circle) is even more deftly rendered, suggesting that Harper Lee has more talent for writing fiction than a number of more famous Pulitzer winners. But nevertheless, *To Kill a Mockingbird* has major defects. The most obvious of these is that the two plots are never really fused or very closely related, except toward the end when they are mechanically hooked together: the trial is over and Tom Robinson dead, but the poor white father of the girl (whom Atticus had exposed in court as a liar and the attempted seductress of Tom Robinson) swears to get revenge. On a dark night, as they are on their way home from a Halloween party, Scout and Jem are waylaid and attacked by the poor white father. Were it not for the timely interference of Boo Radley, Scout and Jem would be murdered. It is then revealed that, from behind his closed shutters, Boo Radley has all along been watching over the lives of the two children who have been trying to invade his privacy. In addition to her failure to achieve an effective structure, the author fails to establish and maintain a consistent point of view. The narrator is sometimes a mature, adult looking back and evaluating events in her childhood. At other times she is a naïve child who fails to understand the implications of her actions. The reason for this inconsistency is that the author has not solved the technical problems raised by her story and whenever she gets into difficulties with one point of view, she switches to the other.

This failure is clearly evident, for instance, during the scene where Scout breaks up a mob of would-be lynchers. This scene is probably the most important section in the novel and it ought to be so convincingly rendered that there will be no doubt in anyone's mind that Scout does the things the author tells us she does. But instead of rendering the actions of Scout and the mob, the author retreats to her naïve point of view. The mob is already gathered before the jail when Scout arrives on the scene. As she looks about, she sees one of her father's clients, Mr. Cunningham, a poor man whose son, Walter, Scout had befriended earlier in the story. When Scout sees Mr. Cunningham she cries, "Don't you remember me, Mr.

Cunningham? I'm Jean Louise Finch." When Mr. Cunningham fails to acknowledge Scout's presence, she mentions Walter's name. Mr. Cunningham is then "moved to a faint nod." Scout remarks, "He did know me, after all." Mr. Cunningham maintains his silence and Scout says, still speaking of his son Walter, "He's in my grade ... and he does right well. He's a good boy ... a really nice boy. We brought him home for dinner one time. Maybe he told you about me ... Tell him hey for me, won't you?" Scout goes on in her innocent way to remind Mr. Cunningham that she and her father have both performed charitable acts for him and Walter, and then the mature narrator breaks in and says, "quite suddenly" that Mr. Cunningham "did a peculiar thing. He squatted down and took me by both shoulders. "I'll tell him you said hey, little lady," he says. Then Mr. Cunningham waves a "big paw" at the other men and calls out, "Let's clear out ... let's get going, boys."[18]

The words "quite suddenly" and "did a peculiar thing" (which are from the point of view of the mature narrator looking back on this scene, and not from that of a naïve little girl as the author evidently wishes us to believe)—these are rhetorical tricks resorted to by fiction writers when they are unable to cope with the difficult problem of rendering a scene dramatically. The author wants Mr. Cunningham to have a change of heart—it is necessary for her story—but she is unable to bring it off dramatically. We are not permitted to see Mr. Cunningham change. The author simply reminds us that Scout befriended Cunningham's son so that we will react sentimentally and attribute our feelings to Mr. Cunningham. Further, the author fails to establish (in this scene as well as earlier) that Mr. Cunningham had any influence over the mob before Scout arrives on the scene. We do not see the mob react to Mr. Cunningham. Such a reaction, had there been one and had it been well done, might convince us that Mr. Cunningham could lead the mob away simply by waving his big paw. As it is, we have to take Scout's supposed power over Mr. Cunningham's emotions and Mr. Cunningham's remarkable power over the mob—on the author's bare assertion.

A third defect in *To Kill a Mockingbird*, this one inherent in the author's simplistic moral, is her sentimental and unreal statement of the Negro problem. Miss Lee is so determined to have her white audience sympathize with Tom Robinson that, instead of making him resemble a human being, she builds him up into a kind of black-faced Sir Galahad, pure hearted and with a withered right arm. Though the author doubtless did not mean to suggest this, her *real* point is that a good Negro (i.e., a handsome, clean-cut, hard-working, selfless, ambitious, family man who knows his place and keeps to it) should not be convicted of a crime he did not commit. Although it is impossible to disagree with this view, nevertheless it does not seem a very significant position to take in 1961. It seems, in fact, not so very different from the stand of T. S. Stribling in 1933. Stribling defended his Negro's right to rise economically on the emotional grounds that he was *really* a white man.

Notes
18. Lee, *To Kill a Mockingbird* (Philadelphia, New York, J. B. Lippincott Co., 1960), 164–65.

CLAUDIA DURST JOHNSON ON UNIVERSAL THEMES

The success of *To Kill a Mockingbird*, one of the most frequently read novels of the last hundred years, can be attributed to its powerful, universal themes. One central theme, encompassing both Part One (which is primarily Boo Radley's story) and Part Two (which is primarily Tom Robinson's story), is that valuable lessons are learned in confronting those who are unlike ourselves and unlike those we know best—what might be called people of difference. In the story, the children must grow up, learn civilizing truths, and rise above the narrowness of the place and time in which private codes and even some legal practices contradict the idealistic principles that the community professes: "Equal rights for all, special privileges for none," as Scout says. In practice, however, equal justice was not available to Boo Radley at that turning point in his life; nor is it available to the Tom Robinsons of this world.

Within such a social climate, the children learn how citizens of their community, which is made up of different races, classes, and temperaments, interact in times of crisis. The "outsiders" in this novel are primarily represented by the unseen eccentric, Boo Radley, and by the African-American, Tom Robinson. They are clearly outside the mainstream of Maycomb society, even though they have lived in the community for as long as most can remember. Because of their position in society, they are at first regarded by the children as demonic and witchlike. But in the process of maturing, the children come to embrace the outsiders among them. Even more, they come to acknowledge their kinship with the outsiders—in a sense, the outsider within themselves.

During the course of the novel, the children pass from innocence to knowledge. They begin to realize their own connection with the community's outsiders, and they observe one man's heroism in the face of community prejudice. One overarching theme of the novel—which brings Part One, the story of Boo Radley and the children, in union with Part Two, the trial of Tom Robinson—can be stated in this way: the mark of virtue, not to mention maturity and civilization, involves having the insight and courage to value human differences— people unlike ourselves and people we might label as outsiders.

In this novel the emphasis is on people of a race and culture different from that of the Finch children, but it also includes the eccentric Boo Radleys of the world who are so different from the people we are and know that they become witchlike and demon-like in the homogeneous community's consciousness. After all, difference is unsettling, even frightening. As the children learn, it takes a strong mind and a big heart to come to love Boo Radley, of whom they are at first so terrified; and it takes immense courage to defend another human being, one who is different from themselves, against community injustice born of fear.

Certainly, as Atticus says in his final summation to the jury, not all outsiders are necessarily good people. Bob Ewell is an example. But the children learn that some outsiders they encounter (like Mayella Ewell) deserve their pity, and that others (like Mrs. Dubose) may be more complex than they at first discern. However, as Atticus also says, they all are human beings. They are also, in some way, victims.

Another element of this same theme, an element that incorporates numerous other characters, is the sympathetic bond that the children begin to acknowledge between themselves and the people who are so different from them. Part of the process of Scout's learning to know Boo Radley and the black people in Maycomb is Scout's coming to feel just how much of an outsider she is herself. As an avid reader, she is a freak in her first-grade class. As a tomboy, she is without little girl friends. As an independent-minded daughter of Atticus Finch, she is the object of brutal ridicule in the genteel ladies' missionary society.

A second theme that runs throughout the novel is that the laws and codes the town of Maycomb professes and lives by are always complex and often contradictory. The idea of law is raised at the start of the novel in the epigraph from Charles Lamb: "Lawyers, I suppose, were children once." The main adult character is a lawyer, and his two children seem destined to be lawyers. They are already at an early age familiar with legal terms. Their African-American housekeeper knows that things are different in the household of a lawyer, and she herself has learned to read from a classic book of law. Part One of the book, which develops the children's initiation into a world much uglier than the one they knew within the protective boundaries of their father's house, is built on legalities and social codes, both law-abiding and law-breaking: Scout's "crime" of entering the first grade already knowing how to read, the long-ago arrest of Boo Radley and his friends for their loud behavior in the public square and Boo's second arrest for stabbing his father in the leg, the threat of lynching Tom Robinson, the charge of rape against him, the "entailments" of Mr. Cunningham, the illegal trespassing of the children on the

Radley property, and the breaking of the hunting and truancy laws by the Ewells.

Most of Part Two is concerned with a trial and takes place in a courtroom. Here, most conversation is about legal matters concerning the constitution of juries and the penalty of death for rape. Finally, at the end of the story, Atticus and the sheriff break the law to protect Boo Radley from jail and from the community's attention after he has saved the children's lives by killing Bob Ewell.

A complication of this second theme is that even though the law should protect from evil and injustice the "mockingbirds" like Tom Robinson and Boo Radley and all those people of difference who are often victims of a homogeneous society, it has finally not been able to do so, mainly because hidden social codes contradict their stated legal and religious principles. For whatever reason, the law has been inadequate to protect Tom, who is sent to prison and gets shot. It has also been inadequate to protect Boo, who is imprisoned by his father after a minor youthful skirmish with the law. And it is not the law that protects the children from Bob Ewell. Ironically, although the novel leads us to deplore the violence of the lynch mob that disrupts law, it is only an act of violence rather than law that protects the children from a literal mad dog and a human mad dog, Bob Ewell.

MONROE FREEDMAN ON THE DIFFICULTY OF ATTICUS FINCH AS A ROLE MODEL

A new ethical role model for lawyers is being promoted in scholarly books, law reviews, and bar journals. His name is Atticus Finch. He looks a lot like Gregory Peck. He is a gentleman. He has character.

"For me," writes a California trial lawyer in the October 1991 issue of the *ABA Journal*, "there is no more compelling role model than Atticus Finch.... Fine citizen, parent and lawyer, Finch ... would remind us that this burden [of meeting a higher standard of behavior and trust] is never too much to bear."

Another commentator, in a November 1990 essay in the *Stanford Law Review*, eulogizes Atticus Finch in a different fashion, but with much the same sense of admiration: "[T]here is no longer a place in America for a lawyer like Atticus Finch. There is nothing for him to do here—nothing he can do. He is a moral character in a world where the role of moral thought has become at best highly ambivalent."

And so on. Atticus Finch, the hero of Harper Lee's novel *To Kill a Mockingbird*, has become the ethical exemplar in articles on topics ranging from military justice to moral theology. If we don't do something fast, lawyers are going to start taking him seriously as someone to emulate. And that would be a bad mistake.

The whole business begins with the idea that understanding and abiding by the rules of ethical conduct is not enough. Rather, it is said, a crucial element that is too often overlooked is "character." The notion of character traces back to what Aristotle called "virtue." The quality of virtue or character is not directly concerned with *doing* the right thing, but rather with *being* the right type of person. That is, the person of character will "naturally" act upon the right principles.

The Appointed Model

Atticus Finch is a lawyer in the small town of Macomb [sic], Ala., in the 1930s. As most readers will remember, in the course of the novel a black man, Tom Robinson, is falsely accused of raping a white woman, who, in fact, had been trying to seduce him. Finch is appointed to defend Robinson.

Finch would prefer not to have been appointed but, recognizing his duty as a member of the bar, he carries out the representation zealously. He even risks his own life to protect Robinson from a lynch mob. As we are told in the book, as well as in recent commentaries on lawyers' ethics, Finch acts as he does because he is a gentleman.

Is Atticus Finch, then, a role model for lawyers? I think not.

In risking his life to save Robinson, Finch is undeniably

admirable. But am I really expected to tell my students that they should emulate Finch by putting themselves between a lynch mob and a client? I may be a staunch proponent of zealous representation, but I can't sell what I won't buy.

It's true that Finch, having been appointed by the court to defend an unpopular client, gives him effective representation. That's an important ethical point, but it is also a relatively small one. And a refusal to accept a court's appointment is punishable by imprisonment for contempt.

What looms much larger for me is Atticus Finch's entire life as a lawyer in Macomb [sic] (which, ironically, is what "character" is all about).

Down with Gentlemen?

Let's go back to the idea of the gentleman. Part of my problem with it is that too many people who have carried that title have given it a bad name. Gentlemen tend to congregate together to exclude others from their company and from their privileges on grounds of race, gender, and religion. In short, the gentleman has too often been part of the problem of social injustice and too seldom part of the solution. Aristotle himself was an elitist who taught that there is a natural aristocracy and that some people are naturally fit to be their slaves.

Consider Finch. He knows that the administration of justice in Macomb [sic], Ala., is racist. He knows that there is a segregated "colored balcony" in the courthouse. He knows, too, that the restrooms in the courthouse are segregated—if, indeed, there is a restroom at all for blacks inside the courthouse.

Finch also goes to segregated restaurants, drinks from segregated water fountains, rides on segregated buses, and sits in a park that may well have a sign announcing "No Dogs or Colored Allowed." Finch is not surprised when Robinson, having been convicted by a bigoted jury, is later shot to death with no less than 17 bullets while making a hopeless attempt to escape from prison to avoid execution.

Even more telling, Atticus Finch instructs his children that the Ku Klux Klan is "a political organization more than anything." (David Duke, can you use a campaign manager who looks like Gregory Peck?) Finch also teaches his children that the leader of the lynch mob is "basically a good man" who "just has his blind spots."

In this respect, Finch is reminiscent of Henry Drinker, author of the first book on the American Bar Association's Canons of Professional Ethics, which governed from 1908 until 1970. In his 1953 book, *Legal Ethics*, Drinker wrestled with what he considered a particularly difficult ethical conundrum: If a lawyer has been convicted of lynching a black man, is the lawyer guilty of a crime involving moral turpitude and therefore subject to disbarment?

Finch also is capable of referring to Eleanor Roosevelt not as a great humanitarian or even as the First Lady but, mockingly, as "the distaff side of the Executive branch in Washington" who is "fond of hurling" the concept of human equality. Finch's daughter, Scout, is at least as intelligent as Jem, but it is Jem who is brought up to understand that, following his father, he will be a lawyer. Scout understands that she will be some gentleman's lady. Toward that end, she is made to put on her pink Sunday dress, shoes, and petticoat and go to tea with the ladies—where she is taunted with the absurd proposition (which she promptly denies) that she might want to become a lawyer.

Beyond Noblesse Oblige

Atticus Finch does, indeed, act heroically in his representation of Robinson. But he does so from an elitist sense of noblesse oblige. Except under compulsion of a court appointment, Finch never attempts to change the racism and sexism that permeate the life of Macomb [sic], Ala. On the contrary, he lives his own life as the passive participant in that pervasive injustice. And that is not my idea of a role model for young lawyers.

Let me put it this way. I would have more respect for Atticus Finch if he had never been compelled by the court to represent Robinson, but if, instead, he had undertaken voluntarily to establish the right of the black citizens of Macomb [sic] to sit freely in their county courthouse. That Atticus Finch would, indeed, have been a model for young lawyers to emulate.

Don't misunderstand. I'm not saying that I would present as role models those truly admirable lawyers who, at great personal sacrifice, have dedicated their entire professional lives to fighting for social injustice. That's too easy to preach and too hard to practice.

Rather, the lawyers we should hold up as role models are those who earn their living in the kinds of practices that most lawyers pursue—corporate, trusts and estates, litigation, even teaching—but who also volunteer a small but significant amount of their time and skiffs to advance social justice. That is the cause that Atticus Finch, a gentleman of character, chose to ignore throughout his legal career.

CALVIN WOODARD ON RACISM AND THE LAW

From a jurisprudential point of view, we can best appreciate *To Kill a Mockingbird*, and its contribution to American law, by recognizing it as an attempt by a critic of the Southern legal system to deal with a serious legal problem through nonlegal means. The serious legal problem was the shockingly unjust treatment Blacks received in Southern courts.

Ms. Lee perceived law as incapable of dealing with the injustices done to Blacks in Southern courts because the injustices were manifestations of a wider, more pervasive problem that affected the whole of Southern society: the ages old problem of racism. Accordingly, she was forced to look beyond law to extralegal means to address what would ordinarily be regarded as a jurisprudential problem: the functions of the legal system.

The need to go beyond law was not without precedent. In other times and places lawyers, judges, scholars, and legal critics have not hesitated, when faced with particularly knotty legal problems, to go outside law—to religion, philosophy, ethics, or the social sciences—for extra-legal authority to justify legal decisions or indeed law itself. So also Ms. Lee: she differed only in that she turned to fiction, specifically to a form of children's literature, to facilitate changes that law itself seemed incapable of bringing about. Ms. Lee's use of fiction, though wonderfully fresh in the jurisprudential context of the 1950s (when she wrote), was not unusual or even uniquely Southern in other contexts.

Ms. Lee was not an "in your face" critic. She did not overtly identify racism as the problem with which she was concerned, nor did she assert her purpose to be the eradication of that problem. She did not even attack Southern law in the more conventional manner of a moral crusade against evil, usually personified by rabid Klansmen, corrupt cops, and know-nothing rednecks. Rather, in the style of a law professor teaching first year law students, she did not "lay out" her purpose. She left it to her readers to think for themselves, to draw their own conclusion by their own powers of reasoning, not by being led by the nose.

The book implies that the real problem in the South was a mystery disease far more subtle and pervasive than the crude brutalities associated with the unsavory characters in the book. Indeed, the worst villains are themselves easily seen as pathetic victims of something larger and more evil than their own venality: they are all victims of the existing social order itself, based on a hallowed tradition sustained by an elaborate network of personal relationships, custom and conventions, and ultimately enforced by law. Together, all these factors sustained a virtually invincible status quo in which racial bias was often so subtle that many white persons vehemently denied that it existed, or even that they were themselves prejudiced against Blacks. Yet, whether they were or not, the cold fact remained: Blacks were held in a subhuman status.

So seen, racism in the South had two distinct dimensions: (i) a cluster of attitudes, shared by Whites, which perpetuated the biased social order; and (ii) the horrid results of the biased social order—one manifestation of which was a legal system where due process of law was consistently denied to nonwhites.

With the exception of the one criminal (rape) trial, however, Ms. Lee wrote about Whites. She details the attitudes and habits of the white folks of Maycomb County, rather than the injustices visited upon Blacks. Until the values of Whites change, she seems to say, society will not change; and, as law reflects the values of society, it can do no more than uphold those values.

To Ms. Lee, "changing white values" was a banner of hope— a way of solving the American dilemma—a way of freeing the South from the dead hand of custom that held the South, and the nation, hostages to its own past.

So much for Ms. Lee's conception of the problem. Her task was a formidable one: how can one possibly hope to alter attitudes touching every aspect of life, and appearing to be as natural as the color of grass? The task she set for herself was not only intellectually difficult, but considering the nature of her purpose, and the hypersensitivity of many Southerners to any criticism of things Southern, it was also fraught with danger. Ms. Lee had good reason to be discreet in her criticisms of the South or things Southern, including Southern law.

Dean Shakelford on Gender Issues

Aunt Alexandra was fanatical on the subject of my attire. I could not possibly hope to be a lady if I wore breeches; when I said I could do nothing in a dress, she said I wasn't supposed to be doing anything that required pants. Aunt Alexandra's vision of my deportment involved playing with small stoves, tea sets, and wearing the Add-A-Pearl necklace she gave me when I was born; furthermore, I should be a ray of sunshine in my father's lonely life. I suggested that one could be a ray of sunshine in pants just as well, but Aunty said that one had to behave like a sunbeam, that I was born good but had grown progressively worse every year. She hurt my feelings and set my teeth permanently on edge, but when I asked

Atticus about it, he said there were already enough sunbeams in the family and to go about my business, he didn't mind me much the way I was.

This passage reveals the importance of female voice and gender issues in Harper Lee's popular Pulitzer Prize-winning novel, *To Kill a Mockingbird*, first published in 1960. The novel portrays a young girl's love for her father and brother and the experience of childhood during the Great Depression in a racist, segregated society which uses superficial and materialistic values to judge outsiders, including the powerful character Boo Radley. [...]

A number of significant questions about gender are raised in the novel: Is Scout (and, by implication, all females) an outsider looking on an adult male world which she knows she will be unable to enter as she grows into womanhood? Is her identification with Atticus due not only to her love and devotion for a father but also to his maleness, a power and freedom she suspects she will not be allowed to possess within the confines of provincial Southern society? Or is her identification with Atticus due to his androgynous nature (playing the role of mother and father to her and demonstrating stereotypically feminine traits: being conciliatory, passive, tolerant, and partially rejecting the traditional masculine admiration for violence, guns, and honor)? All three of these questions may lead to possible, even complementary readings which would explain Scout's extreme identification with her father.

As in the passage quoted at the beginning of this essay, the novel focuses on Scout's tomboyishness as it relates to her developing sense of a female self. Also evident throughout the novel is Scout's devotion to her father's opinions. Atticus seems content with her the way she is; only when others force him to do so does he concern himself with traditional stereotypes of the Southern female. Especially significant with regard to Scout's growing sense of womanhood is the novel's very important character, Aunt Alexandra, Atticus's sister, who is left out of the film entirely. Early in the novel, readers are made aware of Scout's antipathy for her aunt, who wishes to mold her into a Southern lady. Other female authority figures with whom Scout has difficulty agreeing are her first-grade teacher, Miss Fisher, and Calpurnia, the family cook, babysitter, and surrogate mother figure. When the females in authority interfere with Scout's perceptions concerning her father and their relationship, she immediately rebels, a rebellion which Atticus does not usually discourage—signifying her strong identification with male authority and her recognition that the female authority figures threaten the unique relationship which she has with her father and which empowers her as an individual.

Exactly why Scout identifies with Atticus so much may have as much to do with his own individuality and inner strength as the fact that he is a single parent and father. Since the mother of Scout and Jem is dead, Atticus has assumed the full responsibility of playing mother and father whenever possible—though admittedly he employs Calpurnia and allows Alexandra to move in with them to give the children, particularly Scout, a female role model. However, Atticus is far from a stereotypical Southern male. Despite his position as a respected male authority figure in Maycomb, he seems oblivious to traditional expectations concerning masculinity (for himself) and femininity (for Scout). The children in fact see him as rather unmanly: "When Jem and I asked him why he was so old, he said he got started late, which we felt reflected on his abilities and his masculinity." Jem is also upset because Atticus will not play tackle football. Mrs. Dubose criticizes Atticus for not remarrying, which is very possibly a subtle comment on his lack of virility. Later the children learn of his abilities at marksmanship, at bravery in watching the lynch mob ready to attack Tom Robinson, and at the defense of the same man. Perhaps this is Lee's way of suggesting that individuals must be allowed to develop their own sense of self without regard to rigid definitions of gender and social roles.

Scout's identification with Atticus may also be rooted in her recognition of the superficiality and limitations of being a

Southern female. Mrs. Dubose once tells her: "'You should be in a dress and camisole, young lady! You'll grow up waiting on tables if somebody doesn't change your ways ...'" This is one of many instances in the novel through which the first-person narrator reveals Lee's criticism of Southern women and their narrowmindedness concerning gender roles. Even Atticus ridicules the women's attitudes. In one instance he informs Alexandra that he favors "'Southern womanhood as much as anybody, but not for preserving polite fiction at the expense of human life.'" When Scout is "indignant" that women cannot serve on juries, Atticus jokingly says, "'I guess it's to protect our frail ladies from sordid cases like Tom's. Besides ... 'I doubt if we'd ever get a complete case tried—the ladies'd be interrupting to ask questions.'" This seemingly sexist passage may in fact be the opposite; having established clearly that Atticus does not take many Southern codes seriously, Lee recognizes the irony in Atticus's statement that women, including his own independent-minded daughter, are "frail."

Admittedly, few women characters in the novel are very pleasant, with the exceptions of Miss Maudie Atkinson, the Finches' neighbor, and Calpurnia. Through the first-person female voice, Southern women are ridiculed as gossips, provincials, weaklings, extremists, even racists—calling to mind the criticism of Southern manners in the fiction of Flannery O'Connor. Of Scout's superficial Aunt Alexandra, Lee writes: "... Aunt Alexandra was one of the last of her kind: she has river-boat, boardingschool manners; let any moral come along and she would uphold it; she was born in the objective case; she was an incurable gossip." Scout's feelings for Alexandra, who is concerned with family heritage, position, and conformity to traditional gender roles, do alter somewhat as she begins to see Alexandra as a woman who means well and loves her and her father, and as she begins to accept certain aspects of being a Southern female. As Jem and Dill exclude her from their games, Scout gradually learns more about the alien world of being a female through sitting on the porch with Miss Maudie and observing Calpurnia work in the kitchen, which makes her begin "to think there was more skill involved in being a girl" than she has previously thought. Nevertheless, the book makes it clear that the adult Scout, who narrates the novel and who has presumably now assumed the feminine name Jean Louise for good, is still ambivalent at best concerning the traditional Southern lady.

Of special importance with regard to Scout's growing perceptions of herself as a female is the meeting of the missionary society women, a scene which, like Aunt Alexandra's character, is completely omitted from the film. Alexandra sees herself as a grand host. Through observing the missionary women, Scout, in Austenian fashion, is able to satirize the superficialities and prejudices of Southern women with whom she is unwilling to identify in order to become that alien being called woman. Dressed in "my pink Sunday dress, shoes, and a petticoat," Scout attends a meeting shortly after Tom Robinson's death, knowing that her aunt makes her participate as "part of ... her campaign to teach me to be a lady." Commenting on the women, Scout says, "Rather nervous, I took a seat beside Miss Maudie and wondered why ladies put on their hats to go across the street. Ladies in bunches always filled me with vague apprehension and a firm desire to be elsewhere...."

As the meeting begins, the ladies ridicule Scout for frequently wearing pants and inform her that she cannot become a member of the elite, genteel group of Southern ladyhood unless she mends her ways. Miss Stephanie Crawford, the town gossip, mocks Scout by asking her if she wants to grow up to be a lawyer, a comment to which Scout, coached by Aunt Alexandra, says, "Nome, just a lady"—with the obvious social satire evident. Scout clearly does not want to become a lady. Suspicious, Miss Stephanie replies, "'Well, you won't get very far until you start wearing dresses more often.'" Immediately thereafter, Lee exposes even further the provincialism and superficiality of the group's appearance of gentility, piety, and morality. Mrs. Grace Merriwether's comments on "'those poor Mruna'" who live "'in that jungle'" and need Christian salvation reflect a smug, colonialist attitude toward other races. When the women begin conversing about blacks in America, their bigotry—and Scout's disgust with it—becomes obvious.

Rather than the community of gentility and racism represented in the women of Maycomb, Scout clearly prefers the world of her father, as this passage reveals: "... I wondered at the world of women .... There was no doubt about it, I must soon enter this world, where on its surface fragrant ladies rocked slowly, fanned gently, and drank cool water." The female role is far too frivolous and unimportant for Scout to identify with. Furthermore, she says, "But I was more at home in my father's world. People like Mr. Heck Tate did not trap you with innocent questions to make fun of you.... Ladies seemed to live in faint horror of men, seemed unwilling to approve wholeheartedly of them. But I liked them .... [N]o matter how undelectable they were, ... they weren't hypocrites." This obviously idealized and childlike portrayal of men nevertheless gets at the core of Scout's conflict. In a world in which men seem to have the advantages and seem to be more fairminded and less intolerant than women with their petty concerns and superficial dress codes, why should she conform to the notion of Southern ladyhood? Ironically, Scout, unlike the reader, is unable to recognize the effects of female powerlessness which may be largely responsible for the attitudes of Southern ladies. If they cannot control the everyday business and legal affairs of their society, they can at least impose their code of manners and morality.

To Scout, Atticus and his world represent freedom and power. Atticus is the key representative of the male power which Scout wishes to obtain even though she is growing up as a Southern female. More important, Lee demonstrates that Scout is gradually becoming a feminist in the South, for, with the use of first-person narration, she indicates that Scout/Jean Louise still maintains the ambivalence about being a Southern lady she possessed as a child. She seeks to become empowered with the freedoms the men in her society seem to possess without question and without resorting to trivial and superficial concerns such as wearing a dress and appearing genteel.

Harper Lee's fundamental criticism of gender roles for women (and to a lesser extent for men) may be evident especially in her novel's identification with outsider figures such as Tom Robinson, Mayella Ewell, and Boo Radley. Curiously enough, the outsider figures with whom the novelist identifies most are also males. Tom Robinson, the male African American who has been disempowered and annihilated by a fundamentally racist, white male society, and Boo Radley, the reclusive and eccentric neighbor about whom legends of his danger to the fragile Southern society circulate regularly, are the two "mockingbirds" of the title. Ironically, they are unable to mock society's roles for them and as a result take the consequences of living on the margins—Tom, through his death; Boo, through his return to the protection of a desolate isolated existence.

Throughout the novel, however, the female voice has emphasized Scout's growing distance from her provincial Southern society and her identification with her father, a symbol of the empowered. Like her father, Atticus, Scout, too, is unable to be a "mockingbird" of society and as a result, in coming to know Boo Radley as a real human being at novel's end, she recognizes the empowerment of being the other as she consents to remain an outsider unable to accept society's unwillingness to seek and know before it judges. And it is perhaps this element of the female voice in Harper Lee's *To Kill a Mockingbird* which most makes Horton Foote's screen adaptation largely a compromise of the novel's full power.

JOSEPH CRESPINO ON THE LIBERALISM OF ATTICUS FINCH

Part of Atticus Finch's heroic power lies in his ability to embrace the need and the moral imperative for racial change without rejecting his native South. He reminds Scout that though this time they were not fighting against "the Yankees, we're fighting our friends," she should hold no grudges because "no matter how bitter things get, they're still our friends and this is still our home." But in this scene Lee comforts white southerners fearful of the change that was imminent in the South. As Eric Sundquist writes, "Just as the South closed ranks against the nation at the outset of desegregation ... so *To Kill a Mockingbird* carefully narrows the terms on which changed race relations are going to be brought about in the South." Through Atticus Finch, Lee reassured anxious white southerners that civil rights change could come to the South peacefully, without bitterness, and without dividing the white southern community. After all, the southern liberals leading the change were longtime friends and neighbors; they were, first and foremost, southerners.(15) At the same time, for readers North and South who admired the book's racial mores, Atticus represented the continuity of American values of justice and equality. The novel tells us that even in the Depression-era Jim Crow South, the era of Scottsboro and Bilbo, there existed within the South men like Atticus Finch who would be the seeds of the transformation to come. Atticus is a modern hero who, while embodying the most noble aspects of the southern tradition, also transcended the limits of that tradition and attained a liberal, morally rational racial viewpoint that was seen as quintessentially American. Above all, Atticus's morality drives the novel, a morality that is as evident in *To Kill a Mockingbird* as it is in one of American liberalism's signature documents, the Supreme Court's majority decision in *Brown v. Board of Education* (1954). Earl Warren's decision resonated with moral authority: "Such considerations apply with added force to children in grade and high schools. To separate them from others of similar age and qualifications solely because of their race generates a feeling of inferiority as to their status in the community that may affect their hearts and minds in a way unlikely ever to be undone." In *To Kill a Mockingbird* Lee's decision to report Atticus's heroics through the perspective of his nine-year-old daughter is crucial in reinforcing the moral impulse that it is children who ultimately have the most at risk in the nation's struggle to end racial segregation. The project was to be carried out by good liberals like Atticus, but even then it was most effective because it was backed by the moral weight of a child's voice.

THEODORE HOVET AND GRACE-ANN HOVET
ON CONTENDING VOICES

To Kill a Mockingbird (1960) remains an important work because Harper Lee insistently undermines typical assumptions in the United States about the origins of racism. Rather than ascribing racial prejudice primarily to "poor white trash" (Newitz and Wray), Lee demonstrates how issues of gender and class intensify prejudice, silence the voices that might challenge the existing order, and greatly complicate many Americans' conception of the causes of racism and segregation. [...]

The middle-class narrative voice in *To Kill a Mockingbird* which is so appealing to most readers articulates what would become one of the dominant arguments of southern progressives, one uncritically echoed by many northern liberals. What some might see as virulent southern racism, the narrator tries to tell us, is not characteristic of the South as a whole but was created and sustained by a backward element in the rural South represented in the novel by the Ewell clan. Unable or unwilling to employ modern agricultural practices or to educate themselves and their children in modern forms of labor, this "white trash" mistakenly blames its increasingly marginal position in society on the intrusion of African Americans who will not accept their secondary social status. As one of the whites in *To Kill a Mockingbird* puts it, "it's time somebody taught 'em a lesson, they ... gettin' way above themselves" (225). Moreover, Scout explains, these rural whites blame the increasing presence of African Americans on the more prosperous white leadership in the towns—"those bastards who thought they ran this town," to quote Bob Ewell (226). For this reason, the narrator would have us believe, the unjust treatment of African Americans like Tom Robinson is not the fault of the leaders of southern society like her father, the judge, and the newspaper editor. It is the product of an uneducated and irresponsible class of poor whites who use physical intimidation and mob rule to defend what little status they have left. From her vantage point in the late 1950s, the narrator of *To Kill a Mockingbird* implies that this group is an anachronism which will disappear in the wake of an emerging industrialized and urbanized "New South." The Atticus Finches will then assume their rightful leadership positions and begin creating a more just society. The narrator's strategy of placing responsibility for American intolerance and injustice on the vanishing rural poor—what we can call "the white trash scenario"—was so successful that it has become a cliché in popular culture, evident not only in *To Kill a Mockingbird* but also in films like *Easy Rider* and in prime time television programs such as *Heat of the Night* and *I'll Fly Away*.

This is not to say that the narrator and other southern apologists were completely disingenuous. The virulent racism of rural whites helped maintain Jim Crow, fueled the resistance, often violent, to the Civil Rights Movement, and fed the popularity of demagogues like Orville Faubus, Lester Maddox, and George Wallace. The attempt by southern apologists to assign this group the primary responsibility for racism in order to exonerate middle- and upper-class whites, however, is a false reading of history. As C. Vann Woodward pointed out during the early stages of the southern Civil Rights Movement, American imperialism and its slogan of "the white man's burden," along with Supreme Court decisions in the 1890s supporting segregation, implicated the nation as a whole in racist policies. Despite this reality, nevertheless, the white trash scenario worked because the accused were a natural scapegoat. Mostly uneducated and without voice in the media, desperately poor and without economic influence, poor rural whites were helpless to counter the negative stereotype created by the southern apologists and perpetuated by the national media. They were demonized into "the other" by civil rights advocates and progressive southerners. "Poor whites," conclude Annalee Newitz and Matthew Wray in their analysis of white trash, "are stereotyped as virulently racist in comparison with their wealthier counterparts. As long as the poor are said to possess such traits, people can convince themselves that the poor should be cast out of mainstream society ..." (171).

Ironically, Lee's desire to create a realistic portrayal of a southern region unmasked the strategy of the southern apologists, including her own. In order to make southern racism understandable, she not only used the techniques of realism and regionalism, but she also created a double plot, the stories surrounding Boo Radley and Tom Robinson. Several influential critics such as W. J. Stuckey and Harold Bloom maintain that the two stories are a result of artistic failure, an inability to create an organically developed narrative. But, as Claudia Johnson has demonstrated, the double plot opens the text to a more profound reading than one would expect from Lee's use of the "coming of age" or "beset American justice" formulas. Johnson points out that by placing the story of the children's reactions to "Boo," the Finch's neighbor, whom the town thinks is mentally impaired, alongside the town's response to Tom Robinson, Lee makes concrete the psychology of racism. More specifically, Scout and Jem's construction of "Boo" as a gothic monster, an "other" that embodies the mysterious outside forces that constantly threaten the known world of home and family, suggests that white southern society has also constructed the African American as an "other," a monster, who supposedly threatens the established order. Just as Scout and Jem must grow up by confronting the gothic monster of their own and the town's creation, Johnson's reading contends, so must southern society confront the racial monster that it has constructed (*Threatening Boundaries* 67–72).

Works by Harper Lee

To Kill a Mockingbird, 1960.

"Love—In Other Words" (magazine article), 1961.

"Christmas to Me" (magazine article), 1961.

"When Children Discover America" (magazine article), 1965.

"High Romance and Adventure," 1985.

Annotated Bibliography

Adams, Phoebe. "Summer Reading." *Atlantic Monthly:* August 26, 1960, pp. 98–99.

This is an oft-quoted, though brief review, in which Phoebe Adams dismisses *To Kill a Mockingbird* as a typical summer reading novel—pleasant and undemanding.

Barge, R. Mason. "Fictional Characters, Fictional Ethics." *Legal Times:* March 9, 1992.

One of the most heated responses to Monroe Freedman's article "Atticus Finch, Esq., R.I.P." in which the author argues that Freedman is not only unrealistic in his politically conscious expectations, but he unfairly judges Finch by contemporary standards.

Bloom, Harold, (ed.). *Modern Critical Interpretations: Harper Lee's* To Kill a Mockingbird. Chelsea House Publishers: Philadelphia, 1999.

A compendium of full-length essays on *To Kill a Mockingbird*, notably from R.A. Dave, Claudia Durst Johnson, and Fred Erisman, as well as two articles which compare the novel with the film.

Capote, Truman. *Other Voices, Other Rooms.* New York: Random House, 1968.

This is a particularly interesting novel to read and compare with *To Kill a Mockingbird*, as they are written about the same town during the same time. This was Capote's first novel, finished when he was barely twenty, and while Lee's book is orderly and conscionable, *Other Voices, Other Rooms* is gothic mayhem. Lee herself makes an appearance as the tomboy Idabel—not a sweet tomboy like Scout, but a girl who verges on the sadistic.

Carter, Dan T. *Scottsboro: A Tragedy of the American South*, Baton Rouge:Louisiana State University, 1969.

A lucid account of the 1931 trial of nine black men that

allegedly is one of the influences behind the trial of Tom Robinson. It also offers a detailed description of the atmosphere in Alabama around that time.

Clarke, Gerald. *Capote.* New York: Simon and Schuster, 1988.

Though its section on Truman's childhood is brief, it is certainly vivid, with comments on the Lee family and Harper Lee. It also details Lee's later collaboration with Capote on *In Cold Blood.*

Crespino, Joseph. "The Strange Career of Atticus Finch." *Southern Cultures* 6, no. 2, 2000: 9.

Crespino discusses the liberalism of Atticus Finch as the driving force behind the morality in *To Kill a Mockingbird.*

Dave, R.A. "*To Kill a Mockingbird*: Harper Lee's Tragic Vision." *Indian Studies in American Fiction.* Calcutta: The Macmillan Company of India Limited, 1974: 311–323.

Dave discusses the elements of Greek tragedy in *To Kill a Mockingbird*, focusing on such topics as the battle between good and evil, tragic heroes, and unity of place and action.

Erisman, Fred. "The Romantic Regionalism of Harper Lee." *Alabama Review* 26, no. 2, 1973: 126–136.

Erisman asserts that Harper Lee presents a dual view of the South—New and Old—in *To Kill a Mockingbird*, and that the south can no longer stand as a separate entity from the rest of the country.

Ford, Nick Aaron. "Battle of the Books: A Critical Survey of Significant Books by and about Negroes Published in 1960." *Phylon* 22, no. 2, 1961: 122–23.

Ford discusses the role of African Americans in *To Kill a Mockingbird*, asserting that Lee portrayed them in an honest, non-stereotypical way.

Freedman, Monroe. "Atticus Finch—Right and Wrong." *Alabama Law Review* 45, no. 2, 1994: 473–482.

Freedman discusses the moral education of Scout—

especially how she must learn to incorporate the lessons of character from her father with the lessons of the prudence that behooves her gender.

———. "Atticus Finch, Esq., R.I.P." *Legal Times*: February 24, 1992: 20.

In a controversial piece, Freedman argues that Atticus Finch is not a good role model for lawyers.

———. "Finch: The Lawyer Mythologized." *Legal Times:* May 18, 1992: 25.

Freedman responds to the controversy that he provoked with his article "Atticus Finch, Esq., R.I.P."

Going, William T. "Store and Mockingbird: Two Pulitzer Novels about Alabama." Tuscaloosa: University of Alabama Press: *Essays on Alabama Literature*, 1975: 9–31.

Going compares and contrasts T.S. Stribling's *The Store*, which is set in Florence, Alabama, with Lee's *To Kill a Mockingbird*.

Hoff, Timothy. "Influences on Harper Lee: A Introduction to the Symposium." *Alabama Law Review* 45, no. 2, 1994: 389–401.

Hoff discusses Lee's relationship with her childhood friend Capote and its impact on the novel.

Hovet, Theodore and Grace-Ann Hovet. "'Fine Fancy Gentlemen'" and "'Yappy Folk'": Contending Voices in *To Kill a Mockingbird*." *Southern Quarterly* 40, no. 1, 2001: 67–78.

The Hovets demonstrate how issues of class and gender factor in the escalation of prejudice and racism in *To Kill a Mockingbird*.

Johnson, Claudia Durst. To Kill a Mockingbird: *Threatening Boundaries*. New York: Twayne, 1994.

A collection of essays on *To Kill a Mockingbird*, and quite possibly the only widely available book dedicated to the novel.

————.*Understanding* To Kill a Mockingbird: *A Student Casebook to Issues, Sources and Historical Documents.* Westport, CT: Greenwood, 1994.

A highly useful and fascinating assembly of sources which includes interviews with Southern ladies who grew up around the same time as Scout, transcripts from the Scottsboro trials, clips from writers like Faulkner about the plight of the "white trash," and detailed bibliographies throughout.

Johnson, Claudia. "Without Tradition and Within Reason: Judge Horton and Atticus Finch in Court." *Alabama Law Review* 45, no. 2, 1994: 483–510.

Johnson compares Atticus Finch with the real-life Judge Horton, who placed his position in jeopardy when he overturned the guilty verdicts at the Scottsboro trials and ordered a re-trial.

Lemay, Harding. "Children Play; Adults Betray." *The New York Herald Tribune Book Review.* July 10, 1960: 5.

Lemay discusses the interweaving of childhood recollections with the harsher theme of racism in *Mockingbird.*

Moates, Marianne M., *A Bridge of Childhood: Truman Capote's Southern Years.* New York: H. Holt, 1989.

Provides a glimpse of Truman Capote's childhood through the memories of his cousin. There are countless memories of Nelle Harper Lee, as well as anecdotes that are strangely reminiscent of episodes in *Mockingbird.*

Shakelford, Dean. "The Female Voice in *To Kill a Mockingbird*: Narrative Strategies in Film and Novel." *Mississippi Quarterly* 50, no. 1, 1996–1997.

Shakelford discusses the importance of the female voice and gender roles in *To Kill a Mockingbird.*

Stuckey, W.J. *The Pulitzer Prize Novels: A Critical Backward Look*. Norman: University of Oklahoma Press, 1966.

In an excerpt from his book, Stuckey addresses the major defects in *To Kill a Mockingbird*, focusing on the discrepancies between the double plot.

Woodard, Calvin. "Listening to the Mockingbird." *Alabama Law Review* 45, no. 2, 1994: 563–584

Woodard circumnavigates the obvious issue of the role of justice in the novel to attack what is considered the provenance of literary academics—that of symbolism, particularly that of the mockingbird and its relationship to the South.

Contributors

Harold Bloom is Sterling Professor of the Humanities at Yale University and Henry W. and Albert A. Berg Professor of English at the New York University Graduate School. He is the author of over 20 books, including *Shelley's Mythmaking* (1959), *The Visionary Company* (1961), *Blake's Apocalypse* (1963), *Yeats* (1970), *A Map of Misreading* (1975), *Kabbalah and Criticism* (1975), *Agon: Toward a Theory of Revisionism* (1982), *The American Religion* (1992), *The Western Canon* (1994), and *Omens of Millennium: The Gnosis of Angels, Dreams, and Resurrection* (1996). *The Anxiety of Influence* (1973) sets forth Professor Bloom's provocative theory of the literary relationships between the great writers and their predecessors. His most recent books include *Shakespeare: The Invention of the Human* (1998), a 1998 National Book Award finalist, *How to Read and Why* (2000), *Genius: A Mosaic of One Hundred Exemplary Creative Minds* (2002), and *Hamlet: Poem Unlimited* (2003). In 1999, Professor Bloom received the prestigious American Academy of Arts and Letters Gold Medal for Criticism, and in 2002 he received the Catalonia International Prize.

Mei Chin is a writer living in New York City. In addition to this work she has written on Charles Dickens and Anton Chekov.

Harding Lemay was a playwright and an acclaimed television writer who wrote *Inside, Looking Out: A Personal Memoir* (1971), and *Eight Years in Another World* (1981), an account of his writing for soap operas.

Nick Aaron Ford was a leading African-American critic who wrote *The Contemporary Negro Novel: A Study in Race Relations* (1936), *Black Studies: Threat-or-Challenge* (1973), and other works.

Fred Erisman is Lorraine Sherley Professor of Literature Emeritus at Texas Christian University. He is the author of monographs on Frederic Remington (1975) and Tony Hillerman (1989).

R.A. Dave has been the head of the department of English at Sardar Patel University in Vallabh Vidyanagar, India.

William T. Going is the author of *Scanty Plot of Ground: Studies in Victorian Sonnet* (1976) and *Essays on Alabama Literature* (1975).

W.J. Stuckey, former Professor of English at Purdue University, has written a study of Caroline Gordon (1972) and *The Pulitzer Prize Novels: A Critical Backward Look* (1981).

Claudia Durst Johnson is Professor Emeritus of English at the University of Alabama. In addition to her volume on *To Kill a Mockingbird*, she has published *Daily Life in Colonial New England* (2002), and coauthored *The Social Impact of the Novel: A Reference Guide* (2002) with Vernon Johnson.

Monroe Freedman is a member of the faculty at Hofstra University School of Law. Considered a pioneer in the field of legal ethics, his most recent publication is *Understanding Lawyers' Ethics* (2002), co-written with Georgetown Law Professor Abbe Smith.

Calvin Woodard is Professor Emeritus at the University of Virginia School of Law. He has written numerous articles on *To Kill a Mockingbird*.

Dean Shakelford is Associate Professor and Director of Undergraduate Studies in English at Southeast Missouri State University. In addition to his work on *To Kill a Mockingbird*, he teaches courses on American and Multicultural Literature.

Joseph Crespino is a history fellow at George Mason University. He has written articles on politics and the civil rights movement, and his piece, "The Ways Republicans Talk About Race" was published in *The New York Times* (2002).

Theodore Hovet and **Grace-Ann Hovet** are Professor Emeriti of English at the University of Northern Iowa. Theodore has written books and articles on American Literature, and Grace-Ann has written articles on the initiation formula in the novel. They have jointly published several articles together.

Acknowledgments

"Children Play; Adults Betray" by Harding Lemay. From *The New York Herald Tribune Book Review*: July 10, 1960: 5. © 1960 by Harding Lemay. Reprinted by permission.

"Battle of the Books: A Critical Survey of Significant Books by and about Negroes Published 1960" by Nick Aaron Ford. From *Phylon* 22, no. 2 (summer 1961): 122–23. © 1961 by Nick Aaron Ford. Reprinted by permission.

"The Romantic Regionalism of Harper Lee" by Fred Erisman. From *Alabama Review* 26, no. 2, 1973: 46–48. © 1973 by the University of Alabama Press. Reprinted by permission.

"To Kill a Mockingbird: *Harper Lee's Tragic Vision*" by R.A. Dave. From *Indian Studies in American Fiction*. The Macmillan Company of India Limited, 1974: 321–323. © 1974 by R.A. Dave. Reprinted by permission.

"Store and Mockingbird: Two Pulitzer Novels about Alabama" by William T. Going. From *Essays on Alabama Literature*, 1975: 9–31. © 1975 by William T. Going. Reprinted by permission.

The Pulitzer Prize Novels: A Critical Backward Look, 2nd edition, by W.J. Stuckey: 193–196. Copyright © 1981 by the University of Oklahoma Press. First edition © 1966. Reprinted by permission.

Understanding To Kill A Mockingbird: A Student Casebook to Issues, Sources and Historical Documents by Claudia Durst Johnson: 1–5. © 1994 by Greenwood Publishing Group. Reprinted with permission of Greenwood Publishing Group, Inc., Westport, CT.

"Atticus Finch, Esq., R.I.P" by Monroe Freedman. From *Legal Times*: February 24, 1992: 20. © 1992 by Monroe Freedman. Expanded and revised in "Atticus Finch—Right and Wrong." 45 *Alabama Law Review* 473 (1994). Reprinted by permission.

Index

Characters from the book are listed under their first names unless they are known only by last name.

A

Adventures of Huckleberry Finn (Twain), 7, 52
African Americans. *See also* Civil Rights movement; Racism
    Atticus on fair treatment of, 52–53
    book as protest of injustice to, 57–58
    injustices of legal system towards, 13–14, 26–27, 45, 69–71
    portrayal of, 51–53, 62
    social status of, 40, 45–46, 63–64
Alexandra, Aunt (character)
    alliance with Miss Maudie, 33–34, 47–48
    champions Atticus, 33–34
    overview of character, 19
    as Southern lady, 26, 74–75
    tries to make Scout a lady, 26, 46–47, 71–72, 75–76
Aristotle, 66, 67
Arthur Radley. *See* Boo Radley
Atticus Finch (character)
    coverup of Ewell's killing, 36–37, 45
    creed of, 51–53, 77–78
    elitist viewpoint of, 66–69
    on fair treatment of blacks, 52–53
    heroic aspect of, 21
    Lee's father as model for, 12
    liberalism of, 56, 77–78
    overview of character, 17

    prejudice against "white trash," 41, 44, 79–80
    as role model for lawyers, 65–69
    sees victory in trial, 40
    sexist remarks of, 46, 68, 74
    shoots mad dog, 24, 58, 65
    unmanly/androgynous nature of, 21, 72–73
Attorneys, Atticus Finch as role model for, 65–69
Aunt Alexandra. *See* Alexandra, Aunt

B

Bates, Ruby, 15, 45
Bigotry. *See* Prejudice
Black church, visit to, 25–26, 45–46
Blacks. *See* African Americans
Bloom, Harold
    biographical sketch, 88
    sees double plot as flaw, 81
Bob Ewell (character)
    attacks children, 34–36, 60
    as human mad dog, 65
    humiliation of, 39
    overview of character, 19
Boo (Arthur) Radley (character)
    becomes "real person" to children, 37, 77
    model for, 12
    as mystery, 22, 50, 81
    overview of character, 18
    represents threat to society, 81
    saves children from Ewell, 34, 60
    as social outsider, 63–64, 77, 81
Boular, Sonny, 12, 35
Braxton Underwood (character), 38
A Bridge to Childhood (Moates), 35–36, 49